they
shall
be my
people

The Divine Drama from
Genesis to Revelation

they shall be my people

JOHN TIMMER

CRC Publications
Grand Rapids, Michigan

Library of Congress Cataloging-in-Publication Data
Timmer, John, 1927-
    They shall be my people.

    Bibliography: p.
    ISBN 0-933140-82-7
1. Bible—History of Biblical events. 2. God—Biblical teaching. I. Title.
BS635.2.T5   1983   220.9'5   83-15380
Cover Photo: SuperStock

10 9 8 7 6 5 4 3 2 1

I will be their God, and they s

Jeremiah 31:33b

Contents

Preface

They Shall Be My People is both the title of this book and the name of the course in which this book is used as the text. The course, intended for adults, is part of the church education curriculum produced by the Education, Worship, and Evangelism Department of CRC Publications.

Speak of adult church education and most people think of Bible study. Years of adult church school classes have established that association. And that connection is not inappropriate, since the Bible is the sole sourcebook of the Christian faith and the believer's lifelong guide. Yet church education includes courses on Christian doctrine, on church history, on church government, on prayer, on Christian morality. Of course, all such specialized studies are based on and formed by what the Bible teaches about these matters. So we come back to biblical study as the key to all education in the church of Christ.

They Shall Be My People is a survey of the Bible. Some surveys outline the historical order of dates, names, and events, placing them in proper sequence. Other surveys bare the bones structuring the body, sketching the interrelationships between main teachings and occurrences. Still other surveys view the Bible in its entirety, trying to see the sense of the whole, striving to catch the spirit that permeates it all. They Shall Be My People is a survey in this last sense.

We typically tend to read and study the Bible in small segments: a text, a passage, a chapter, or at most a book. But the Bible is a single book with a single author telling a single story. It is one Word of God. It should be read and understood, first of all, in terms of that oneness. Accordingly, this survey takes large segments of the Bible and presents them in the context of the entire Word of God. It should be read and understood, first of all, in terms of that oneness. It asks and answers the question, "How does this part fit in with the whole of God's written revelation? What does it contribute to the entire revelation of God's grace?"

The author, John Timmer, was born in Haarlem, the Netherlands, and came to the United States to study theology. A graduate of Calvin College and Seminary, he also pursued doctoral studies at Hartford Theological Seminary before receiving his doctoral degree in New Testament studies from the Free

University of Amsterdam. Rev. Timmer was a missionary of the Christian Reformed Church in Japan for fourteen years. He served as pastor of Woodlawn Christian Reformed Church in Grand Rapids, Michigan, until his retirement in 1995.

The author's missionary experience is manifest in his understanding of the entire Bible. He views it as the book of God's gracious covenant and kingly rule—a covenant and kingdom that always keep in view the people who are not yet "my people" and the lands and people where that kingdom has not yet been established.

The questions and Bible studies at the end of his chapters can serve as the basis for an adult or young adult church school class. A leader's guide, also written by Timmer, is available.

We trust this book and this course will deepen your understanding of God's Word and your commitment to live by the light of that Word from day to day.

Harvey A. Smit
Education, Worship, and Evangelism Department

Prologue: Creation

The Bible presents itself to us the same way Jesus presents himself to unbelieving Thomas. Jesus meets Thomas's unbelief halfway. He invites Thomas to touch the scars of his crucifixion. It's as though Jesus tells Thomas, "You have dismissed the news of my resurrection, which came to you through the reports of the other disciples. But here I am myself. See and touch!" And then Thomas surrenders.

In the same way, the Bible invites us to a face-to-face confrontation. It wants to speak to us directly. It wants the opportunity to surrender its secret and prevail over us.

In the chapters that follow I hope to cultivate an awareness of the Scriptures as a single book from whose various parts issues this invitation of the risen Christ: "See and touch!"

The Good News of Genesis 1

To understand Genesis 1 requires a key. The key is John 3:16: "God so loved the world that he gave his one and only Son." God's relationship to the world is not one of cold indifference or unpredictable playfulness. It is one of love. The God who created us is also the God who loves us. We were not created by a malicious god. Nor did we come about by mere chance. We were created by the Father of Jesus Christ. Knowing that makes all the difference in the world.

Only when we open Genesis 1 with the key of John 3:16 can we solve, for example, the problem of how our Christian faith relates to science. When science tells us that our world is five billion years old and that life on earth has existed for some two billion years and that human life is at least half a million years old, we need not be disturbed or feel lost among the staggering numbers of years in geology and biology. Christ, after all, does not meet us in the billions of years it took the universe to become what it now is. Christ does not meet us in the infinity of cosmic years but in the history of Israel. That history reveals to us that God loves the world in Jesus Christ.

Genesis 1 does not answer the question, "In what time sequence and by what process did the world come into being?" The question it answers is this: "Where does the history of Israel really begin?"

Genesis 1 speaks of the beginning. But the beginning of what? The beginning of a cosmic conflict between God and God's archenemy. It is this conflict that makes creation what it now is. Creation is the first chapter of a conflict—the conflict between God and his adversary, the conflict between the power of order and the power of chaos.

Genesis 1 is like a TV set and John 3:16 like the power button. Having pushed that button, what picture appears on the screen? A picture of hope. Genesis 1 invites us to put our trust in the God who is stronger than the powers of chaos. It assures us that chaos does not have the final word, even though for a while it poses a real threat.

In the beginning the earth was inhospitable and uninhabitable. Darkness and the waters made any kind of life impossible. Where do the darkness and the waters come from?

We don't know because we aren't told. Darkness and the waters are just unexplainably there. They were not brought forth the way light and dry land were brought forth, by an express command of God. Darkness and the waters are forces inimical to God's creative purposes, forces operating on the fringes of creation, from which they seek to penetrate and destroy the created order.

Do you wish to know what our world would look like if chaotic forces had penetrated and destroyed it? Then read Jeremiah 4:23-26: "I looked at the earth, and it was formless and empty; and at the heavens, and their light was gone. . . . I looked, and the fruitful land was a desert; all its towns lay in ruins before the LORD, before his fierce anger." Chaos, Jeremiah says, puts creation in reverse. Light makes place for darkness, fruitful land turns into desert, civilization turns into dust.

Genesis 1 provides an exit from this chaotic landscape. It presents a picture of hope. "God said, 'Let there be light,' and there was light. God saw that the light was good, and he separated the light from the darkness." Still, even though at creation the light ousted the darkness, the light did not decisively defeat the darkness. That would happen later, in Revelation 21. For the time being, the darkness remains, but beyond the boundaries God sets for it on this first day of creation.

On the second day God continues to make the world safe from the powers of chaos. God says, "Let there be an expanse between the waters to separate water from water," to separate the lower, terrestrial ocean from the upper, celestial ocean. This expanse, according to the worldview of Old Testament days, holds back the upper ocean, which would otherwise destroy all life on earth, the way it did at the time of the Flood.

On the third and fourth day God's creative Word drives back the darkness and the waters even farther. The dry land appears and God places lights in the expanse to separate the day from the night.

On the fifth day God creates the fish and the birds—creatures that populate the wide spaces between order and chaos. The birds populate the space between the dry land and the ocean above the expanse. The fish populate the space between the dry land and the chaotic waters beyond the horizon.

Genesis 1, in other words, paints a picture of the world that is at the same time frightening and liberating. The universe through which our planet floats is hostile and full of death. Powers that destroy and kill are all around us. But God, in his great mercy and through his creative Word, establishes a realm in the middle of these destructive forces where we can freely breathe. This is the good news Genesis 1 proclaims. God, by his creative Word, keeps us from the terror of night, the arrow that flies by day, the pestilence that stalks in the darkness, and the plague that destroys at midday (Ps. 91:5-6).

Creation and the Exodus

Creation in Genesis 1 is actually a cosmic version of the Exodus, when God led his people through the Red Sea with a wall of water on either side. What happened at creation is what happened at the Exodus. God divided the waters so that the people might walk on dry ground in the midst of destructive waters.

Creation, in the deepest biblical sense, is liberation. By the grace of God we are living inside the big air bubble situated between the terrestrial ocean and the celestial ocean above the expanse. The only thing that keeps us from perishing is the Word of God holding up that expanse.

Genesis 1 tells us this message: outside the realm of God's Word there is no freedom and security anywhere. Desolation, destruction, and death are the final toll we must pay for closing our ears to the Word of God. Life offers two alternatives: obedience to the Word of God or abandonment to the powers of chaos.

There will come a time, the Bible promises, when the powers of chaos will either disappear or turn from an enemy into a friend. There will come a time, the book of Revelation says, when there will be no need for sun and moon to shine, when the terrestrial sea will be no more, and when the celestial sea— the waters above the expanse—will turn into a sea of glass, like crystal. No longer will it be a threat. Rather, it will be an object of delight, a sea of crystal. And because crystal is transparent, it will allow a vision of God. Between the world of Genesis 1 and that of Revelation, however, lies the whole history of Israel. That history is the subject of this book.

Prologue: Creation

Chapter Review Questions

1. What theme is central to Genesis 1?

2. Does the language of creation and chaos sound strange to you? Why or why not?

3. Could you translate the terms "darkness" and "the waters" into everyday language? You may want to read such New Testament passages as Galatians 5:19-21, Ephesians 5:3-5, and Colossians 3:5-9.

4. How does the story told in Revelation 12 relate to the conflict in Genesis 1?

5. In what ways is John 3:16 the key to Genesis 1? See also Numbers 21.

6. How does Jeremiah 4:23-26 describe the invasion of chaos?

7. How does the story of creation resemble the story of Israel's exodus from Egypt?

General Discussion Questions

1. What do you hope to gain from this survey of the Bible?

2. The Prologue ignores an issue that causes many people great concern: How can Christians reconcile scientific theories about the origin of the universe with the biblical account of creation? Is this a serious omission? Why do you suppose the author does not discuss this issue?

3. What understanding of the structure of the universe lies behind Genesis 1? See Psalm 24:2; Job 9:6; 38:6; Psalm 104:5; Jonah 2:6; Genesis 1:8; Proverbs 8:27; Job 37:18; Psalm 148:4; Isaiah 24:18; Psalm 78:23; Genesis 7:11; Isaiah 40:22; Amos 9:6; Psalm 104:3.

Notes

One: God Makes a Promise

Sin Breaks In

In Genesis 3 the serpent engages Eve in a conversation. "Did God say . . . ?" "No," Eve replies, "that's not what he said. What he said was . . . " "But why did God say that?" the serpent asks again. "Did he not say it out of envy? Be intelligent! Be more intelligent than God! What God said is not true. You will not die when you eat of the fruit of the tree which is in the midst of the garden."

What is the serpent telling Eve? That when you disobey God, you are in a better position to know God than when you obey him. That when you step outside the confines of what God has commanded, your life will be richer than when you stay within these confines.

Human folly lies in thinking that God can be understood better from a position of disobedience than from a position of obedience.

Sin Breaks Out

If Genesis 3 describes how sin broke in, Genesis 4-11 describes how sin broke out, causing a total dislocation of human life. No sooner did people turn away from God than they began to picture themselves as powerful even compared to God. In this development toward ever greater disobedience, the book of Genesis points out important milestones: the murder of Abel, Lamech's revenge, the intermarriage of the sons of God with the daughters of humans, the Flood, and the confusion of languages. Each of these stories highlights a different form of rebellion against God, and with each successive story human sin assumes larger proportions.

In Genesis 3 people disobey God for the first time.

In Genesis 4:1-16 a man takes the life of a fellow human being, and thereby infringes upon God's exclusive right—life belongs to him alone. In this story sin invades the social realm. God's question is not, as it was in Paradise, "Where are you?" (Gen. 3:9), but, in keeping with the social nature of Cain's sin, "Where is your brother Abel?"

In Genesis 4:23-24, the so-called Song of Lamech, human sinfulness increases still further. The execution of vengeance—God's exclusive right—here is claimed defiantly by a man: "If Cain is avenged seven times, then Lamech seventy-seven times."

Genesis 6:1-4 describes how the very decrees by which God had separated the sons of God from the daughters of humans are broken and how, in the form of intermarriage, dissolution invades the human community.

This brings us to Genesis 6-8, the story of the Flood. Here human depravity reaches a new peak. "Every inclination of the thoughts of his heart was only evil all the time" (Gen. 6:5). The earth, originally pronounced good, is "corrupt in God's sight" (Gen. 6:11).

After the Flood, human sin increases again when people say, "Let us build ourselves a city, with a tower that reaches to the heavens, so that we may make a name for ourselves" (Gen. 11:4).

The builders intend to measure their accomplishments—city and tower— against God in heaven. The city and tower together symbolize the effort of rebellious people to transcend their divinely appointed limitations. By their cultural achievements they seek to claim equality with God. They wish to be wholly separated from God. As such, their resolve expresses "the ultimate act of rebellion—the total denial of God in the absolute assumption of self-sufficiency. This is sin in totality, with finality" (B. Davie Napier, *From Faith to Faith,* p. 56).

The story of Babel forms the closing event of Israel's prehistory. With the confusion of the common language and the scattering of the people across the face of the earth, God's judgment upon the people of the world appears to be total.

Genesis 3-11 show how a humanity that turns away from God destroys itself, how stepping beyond the boundaries God has created leads to societal suicide. What is going to become of this humanity? Who will save it from destruction?

Genesis 12 provides the answer to these questions. In this chapter, world history makes contact with salvation history. God calls Abraham out of the nations of the world and promises him that all the peoples on earth will be blessed in him.

The opening words of salvation history, therefore, provide the answer to the problem posed by the preceding history of the human race. In Abraham, Israel will be blessed, and through Israel, all nations on earth will be blessed. The purpose in calling Abraham and Israel is to bridge the gulf between God and the entire human race.

The story of Abraham and Israel, which begins in Genesis 12, is but a story within the context of a larger story. The Bible deals first with the world before it deals with Israel and the church. Its message is directed toward the salvation of all of humankind. The first eleven chapters of the Bible speak of the world's farthest bounds, of the origin and destiny of all of humanity.

God Makes a Promise

In the story of the Tower of Babel, the expression "scattered over the face of the whole earth" occurs no less than three times (Gen. 11:4, 8, 9). With

Genesis 12 the field of vision is abruptly narrowed. Suddenly one single man, Abraham, is introduced. With Abraham God begins something new in history: God proceeds to deal with the world, not directly, but indirectly—through Abraham. From this point on the Bible deals only with the history of Abraham and his promised posterity. Still, the main concern of the Bible remains creation and humanity. God still rules over what happens in the world, but in dealing with the world, God works out his purpose through the call of one man and one nation and one mediator. It is through them that his work on behalf of the world reaches its goal.

In Genesis 12 God promises Abraham three things:

1. Abraham will become a great nation (v. 2).
2. God will give land to Abraham's posterity (v. 7).
3. Through Abraham all peoples on earth will be blessed (v. 3).

The first two of these promises, important as they may be, are subordinate to the third promise—the promise of worldwide blessing. In this third promise Israel is told about the reason for its election. Posterity and land are necessary for historical existence and survival. But they are not ends in themselves. Israel's primary mission in history, the purpose of its existence, is to be "a light for the Gentiles" (Isa. 42:6). Israel, however, tended to lose sight of its mission. This we learn, for example, from the book of Jonah. This book was written after the people of Israel had returned from exile in Babylon and after they had been reorganized into a nation by Nehemiah and Ezra and their successors.

This process of nation building had been so thorough that it had made Israel's outlook very narrow and exclusive. Israel increasingly thought of itself as the only nation in the world God cared about. It even looked forward to a time when God would destroy all its enemies and would raise up a powerful Messiah king who would rule over the whole world. Israel had lost sight of its mission to bring the true knowledge of God to the peoples of the earth.

The book of Jonah was written to remind the people of Israel of their missionary calling and to rebuke them: their desire for vengeance made them unfit for service. Jonah, in his experiences, reenacts the experiences of his people, whom he represents. As he flees his mission, so do they. As he looks forward to seeing the Gentiles destroyed, so do they.

The book of Jonah is not the story of a man who survives three days in the stomach of a fish. It is the story of a prophet who makes the staggering discovery that God loves the whole world and that the primary mission of his nation consists in being "a light for the Gentiles."

Will God Keep His Promise?

After telling the story of God's call to Abraham, the book of Genesis addresses itself to this one question: Can, or will, God keep his promise that from Abraham will come forth the servant people of God—Israel, the church? Will God be faithful to his promise? The remainder of the book of Genesis is entirely devoted to answering this question. The stories it tells reflect much doubt and uncertainty about the outcome. They also reflect much compromise and shrewd calculation by people who are distrustful of God's promise and think they have a better way. Genesis 12-50 contains three groups of stories:

The Abraham Stories

Abraham's distrust. "When Christ calls a man," writes Dietrich Bonhoeffer, "he bids him come and die." These words also apply to Abraham. When God calls Abraham, he asks him to give up his country, his clan, and his home (Gen. 12:1). To go where? To the land that God will show him. But when Abraham arrives in that land, the first thing he meets is famine (Gen. 12:10). Hunger forces him to travel to Egypt, where he surrenders his wife to Pharaoh. The surrender of Sarah to another man is the first incident recorded about Abraham after he has received the promise of God into his life. How does Abraham receive the promise of God? He fails the first test.

Why did God choose Abraham? Not because Abraham is honest and truthful. For Abraham lies to Pharaoh to save his life. "Say you are my sister," he instructs Sarah, "so that . . . my life will be spared because of you" (Gen. 12:13). Far from being a morally upright person, Abraham is a liar who stands before Pharaoh selling his wife into Pharaoh's harem. Abraham, therefore, does not merit God's election. Nonelected Pharaoh is more virtuous than elected Abraham. Asks Pharaoh, "Why did you say, 'She is my sister' . . . ? Now then, here is your wife. Take her and go!" (Gen. 12:18-19).

Eight chapters later, in Genesis 20, Abraham repeats the same lie. This time the scene is not Egypt but Gerar. Again Abraham says of Sarah his wife, "She is my sister" (v. 2). Again Sarah is taken into a harem. Again God intervenes to make sure that there will be a mother to bring forth the elect people.

The same plot appears again in Genesis 26:6-11. This time the lying patriarch is Isaac, Abraham's son.

Abraham and Isaac—both take matters into their own hands. Both try to force the fulfillment of God's promise by devious ways and means. Both fear the power of kings more than they trust the promise of God.

God's faithfulness. In Genesis 15:8, Abraham expresses doubt that God will fulfill the promise about the land. "O Sovereign LORD, how can I know that I will gain possession of it?"

God's answer is a ritual of covenant making. Five different animals are cut in half and the pieces laid opposite each other. Custom dictated that the partners to the covenant would then walk through the lane that had been formed by the pieces of meat, expressing thereby a curse upon themselves in the event the covenant was broken. In this case, however, one of the covenant partners is completely passive. A deep sleep falls on Abraham. So does "a thick and dreadful darkness" (Gen. 15:12). In this darkness Abraham sees a smoking pot and a flaming torch pass between the pieces of animal meat.

What does this vision mean? That in the case of God and Abraham the covenant is concluded with the complete passivity of the human partner. "The flame passing between the animals means that God takes upon himself the full weight of the covenant. Abram is not requested to pass between them. Not only the initiation but the fulfillment of the covenant lies in God's hand" (Suzanne de Dietrich, *The Witnessing Community*, p. 35).

Sarah's barrenness. Will there be an heir to the promise God made to Abraham? Will Abraham indeed become a great nation? Will a child be born of Abraham and Sarah?

In utter desperation over the uncertain answer, and following accepted Bronze Age customs, Sarah decides to lend God a helping hand. She commends to Abraham her maid: the Egyptian Hagar. And Hagar bears for Abraham the Arab Ishmael, who, according to the laws and customs of the times, might have become the heir of Abraham and hence the recipient of God's promise. This would have made the Arabs, rather than Israel, the people of God.

Again, God intervenes. He tells Abraham that Sarah will bear him a son. How does Abraham react? At the announcement, "Abraham fell face down . . ." (Gen. 17:17). This is an idiomatic expression. When, in the Old Testament, someone falls face down, the next thing that person does is worship God. Therefore, we expect to read the following: "Then Abraham fell face down and worshiped the Lord." What we read instead is: "Abraham fell face down he laughed and said to himself, 'Will a son be born to a man a hundred years old? Will Sarah bear a child at the age of ninety?' "

Abraham then proceeds to plead for what is biologically possible: "If only Ishmael might live under your blessing!" (Gen. 17:18). In other words, why not fulfill your promise through the Arab Ishmael?

Abraham laughs and Sarah laughs too (Gen. 18:12). Because they do, God tells them that their child's name will be Isaac, which means "he laughs." This is to remind the parents that God is quite capable of fulfilling his promise without the benefit of their advice and assistance.

The binding of Isaac. In Judaism, Genesis 22:1-19 is known as the *Akedah* or "Binding," that is, the binding of Isaac to the altar. The word *Akedah* means not only the binding of Isaac for the sacrifice, but also the binding of God to his people.

This *Akedah* story shocks us into realizing that Israel owes its existence entirely to God and not to Isaac, who is God's gift. Abraham loves Isaac. In doing so he is right. But he is wrong if he thinks that the promise of God hinges on Isaac.

What if Isaac is killed? Will that end all? What if Abraham's knife comes down? Will God's promise then perish with Isaac? We know the answer. God, not Isaac, is the guarantor of the promise. Even if Abraham's knife does kill Isaac, God's cause will not die with Isaac. "By faith Abraham . . . offered Isaac. . . . Abraham reasoned that God could raise the dead" (Heb. 11:17-19).

Looking beyond Genesis and the Old Testament, we see that eventually that knife does come down . . . on Jesus. So strong are the demonic forces opposing the fulfillment of God's promise to Abraham that they kill God's only Son, whom he loves. But so powerful is God, so determined is God to live up to his promise, that on the third day he raises Jesus from the dead.

The Jacob Stories

The Jacob stories, too, inform us that Israel's election is not earned, but the free choice of God. In two ways they emphasize that Israel is God's chosen people, not by virtue of its behavior, but by virtue of God's grace.

In the choice of the younger son. In the ancient Near East, preeminence was naturally given to the older or eldest son. In the Jacob stories, however, God's electing grace upsets and cuts across this cultural expectation. Not the older Esau but the younger Jacob becomes the recipient of Isaac's greatest blessing and of God's promise.

According to the customs of the times, Isaac's blessing could only be transmitted through one line—the line of Esau, the firstborn. God, however, refuses to follow those customs. God, not people, decides how the stream of divine blessing shall flow through history. God ever remains the sovereign dispenser of grace. God always is gracious to whom he chooses to be gracious.

Many Christians err in interpreting the patriarchal stories moralistically and holding up the patriarchs as models. Weigh Jacob and Esau on the moral balances. Jacob is a go-getter. He is determined to make a smashing success of life, at whatever cost. Esau, on the other hand, is strong, but kind. Though wounded, he is tolerant. He does not hold a grudge. He is truthful. But watch out for sneaky Jacob!

The struggle between Jacob and Esau is not a moral struggle between good and evil. Rather, their struggle is between two rivals fighting for God's blessing.

The struggle reaches a climax in Genesis 27, when Isaac feels his end approaching and desires to pass on the blessing to Esau. Naturally! Jacob, however, cheats his brother out of the family birthright and deceives his father into giving him, and not Esau, the blessing of the firstborn.

Those whom God chooses are not morally superior to those who are not chosen. God blesses Jacob, not because of what Jacob is, but because of who God is—one who has mercy on whom he chooses to have mercy.

In the realistic portrayal of Jacob. Throughout the Jacob stories you find a tension between human deviousness and divine purpose, between human sin and divine grace. In and of himself Jacob is treacherous, deceitful, acquisitive, proud, and self-centered. From the realism with which he is portrayed it is obvious that his election is not morally earned. The story of his life is supported entirely by divine grace and purpose. It presents a man laid hold of by God's promise. But Jacob does not carry the promise; the promise carries him, lifting him over all of his sins and failures, which are laid out for everyone to see. Already we are beginning to guess why Christ stands at journey's end.

The Joseph Stories

The Joseph stories take up almost the last quarter of the book of Genesis. What point do they make? What basic question do they answer? Why does Joseph give his brothers such a hard time? Why does he insist that they bring Benjamin with them to Egypt? Why does he command the steward of his house to put the silver cup, Joseph's cup, in the mouth of Benjamin's sack (Gen. 44:1-2)? What motivates Joseph to do all these things?

His motivation stems from his insight into God's design! He has the ability to see in all that has happened the working of God's overruling power.

Joseph claims such insight on two occasions: first when he reveals his identity to his brothers, and again after Jacob dies. The two speeches made on these occasions contain the key that unlocks the meaning of the Joseph stories.

In his first speech Joseph says to his brothers: "God sent me ahead of you to preserve for you a remnant on earth and to save your lives by a great deliverance. So then, it was not you who sent me here, but God" (Gen. 45:7f.). Here Joseph lifts the veil. Here he states the main theme of his life's story: God bends all of human guilt to his gracious purpose.

In the second speech, given shortly after Jacob's death, Joseph speaks similar words: "Don't be afraid. Am I in the place of God? You intended to harm me, but God intended it for good to accomplish what is now being done, the saving of many lives" (Gen. 50:19f.).

God incorporate the evil of his chosen people into his saving activities. Through the evil plots of the brothers, God moved Joseph into a spot where he became responsible for saving the lives, not only of Jacob and his family, but of the whole world (Gen. 41:57).

Genesis 41 reports that there was a famine in every country. Only in Egypt there was grain. "And all the countries came to Egypt to buy grain from Joseph, because the famine was severe in the world" (Gen. 41:57). Through Joseph all the countries are fed. Through Joseph all the peoples on earth are blessed, in direct fulfillment of God's promise to Abraham in Genesis 21:3.

One: God Makes a Promise

Chapter Review Questions

1. What myth does the serpent use to mislead Eve?

2. What crescendo marks the stories in Genesis 3-11?

3. How does Genesis 12 answer the problems of Genesis 3-11?

4. What does God promise Abraham? What other nations or groups have claimed to be specially chosen by God?

5. Which basic question controls the entire book of Genesis?

6. Why does the book of Genesis make so much of Abraham's moral failures?

7. Why does the book of Genesis make so much of Sarah's barrenness?

8. How do the Jacob stories emphasize that election is not earned?

9. How does Joseph live out his election?

General Discussion Questions

1. How is Abraham the model of all believers?

2. How does Abraham's election work itself out in the case of Sodom (see Gen. 18)?

3. How does Abraham's election come to expression in the story of Isaac's sacrifice (see Gen. 22:16-18)?

4. Comment on the following: "Election is like computer software. God is like a computer programmer. I spill coffee on my pants? I win the lottery? I get pregnant? I total my car? Everything that happens has been programmed. At my conception, God programmed me with software. And just as a computer has no control over the software downloaded into it, so I have no control over the kind of program God put into me." What do you think of this notion of election?

5. What is the purpose of election? In other words, what does it mean to you to be chosen or elected in Christ?

6. How is election a story rather than a doctrine? Does this view of election comfort you?

7. In most cases, a book is written over a brief span of time, has a single identified author and a uniform style, and leads up to a climax. Does this also describe the book of Genesis?

Notes

Two: God Names Himself

T he book of Exodus ties in with the dramatic sequence of events in the book of Genesis. The God who addresses Moses is none other than "the God of Abraham, the God of Isaac, and the God of Jacob" (Ex. 3:6). The God who liberates Israel from Egyptian slavery is the same God who intends to bless all peoples on earth through Abraham.

God Names Himself to Moses

God introduces himself to Moses as the God of the fathers who is moved by the plight of his people and who can't wait to become involved in their predicament. "I have indeed seen the misery of my people in Egypt. I have heard them crying out because of their slave drivers, and I am concerned about their suffering. So I have come down to rescue them from the hand of the Egyptians and to bring them up out of that land into a good and spacious land, a land flowing with milk and honey" (Ex. 3:7f.).

Moses, however, is reluctant to go back to Egypt. What, he asks, shall I say to the people of Israel when they ask me, "What is the name of the God who has sent you to us?" God then tells him, "I AM WHO I AM. . . . Say to the Israelites, 'I AM has sent me to you' " (Ex. 3:14).

What is the meaning of the people's question? They certainly want to know more than God's personal name. In the ancient world a personal name was not just a label, as it usually is for us. A person's name was believed to be a disclosure of the inner self. To know a person's name was the same as having a measure of control over that person. By invoking a person's name, one could either bless or curse her. The question, "What is his name?" is asked not so much for God's sake, so that the people might worship him, but far more for their own sake, so that they might enlist God in their own service and bind him to themselves.

God's answer to Moses is puzzling: "I AM WHO I AM." "I AM WHO I AM" is first of all a promise: I will be what I will be. I will be in the future what I was in the past. I will be the same God to you as I was to Abraham, to Isaac, and to Jacob.

'I AM WHO I AM" is not only a promise. It is also an evasion. It means: I am a hidden God, a mysterious God. I am the kind of God you read about in the book of Job—a God whose wisdom is unfathomable and whose thoughts are higher than heaven and deeper than Sheol. "I AM WHO I AM" means: I will be with you wherever you go, but in ways beyond your grasping. I am hidden, yet close; past finding out, yet ever faithful; baffling, yet sustaining. I am always with you, but always on my terms, never on yours.

What the name "I AM WHO I AM" means is beautifully illustrated by the story of the aged Jacob blessing Manasseh and Ephraim—Joseph's two sons. Joseph positions the two boys in such a way that Jacob's right hand—the hand bestowing the greater blessing—will rest on the head of Manasseh, Joseph's firstborn, and his left hand—the hand bestowing the lesser blessing—on the head of Ephraim, Joseph's second-born son. Jacob, however, crosses his arms and lays his right hand on Ephraim's head. Joseph, sure that his father has made a mistake, corrects him. "No, my father, this one is the firstborn; put your right hand on his head" (Gen. 48:18). But Jacob persists. "I know, my son, I know." What is it the blind Jacob knows? He knows that God's freedom cuts across human customs and traditions and that God, in his sovereign freedom, is gracious to whom he chooses to be gracious.

God Reveals Himself to Egypt

Let My People Go!

When God orders Pharaoh to let his people go, he breaks five centuries of silence to the world. The last time God had directly concerned himself with the world was in Genesis 11, when he had said, "Come, let us go down and confuse their language so they will not understand each other." With these words God had taken leave of the peoples of the earth. The next time he speaks is in Genesis 12:1, when he calls Abraham. From now on, God's immediate concern is Abraham and his descendants. God will get back to the peoples of the earth later. But first he is going to fashion himself a servant people.

Moses is the first one in the long row of spokespersons who, representing this servant people, address the people of the world on God's behalf. Standing before Pharaoh, Moses breaks God's centuries-long silence by commanding: Let God's people go!

At first hearing, these words sound unreasonable. After all, owning slaves in the ancient world was perfectly legal. Why then should Pharaoh not be allowed to own Hebrew slaves? The answer: because Israel is God's firstborn son, and God, as father, has a perfect right under ancient law to demand back his son from the tyrant who enslaves him. God's demand to Pharaoh, "Israel is my firstborn son, and I told you, 'Let my son go, so he may worship me.' But you refused to let him go; so I will kill your firstborn son" (Ex. 4:22f.), is in precise accordance with the social laws and customs of that time. By not letting Israel go, Pharaoh is flouting established social regulations; and God is intervening, "Not like a despot, but in the faithful exercise of a recognized privilege" (David Daube, *The Exodus Pattern in the Bible*, p. 13).

"Let my people go!" These words may also sound as though God is concerned only with liberating the Hebrews and not the Egyptians. But this is not true, for God's word to Pharaoh is: "Israel is my firstborn son." The fact that God calls Israel his firstborn son, writes George A. F. Knight, is of great theological importance. "The firstborn was set apart for the service both of God and of God's other sons and daughters. When God adopted Israel, all other nations of men ipso facto became God's children too" *(Theology as Narration, p. 34).*

God chose Israel, not to receive special privileges, but to bear special responsibilities. Which ones? To be "a light for the Gentiles," that God's salvation might reach "to the ends of the earth" (Isa. 49:6).

Pharaoh Hardens His Heart

The book of Exodus characterizes Pharaoh's response to God's demand as "hardness of heart." It mentions this no less than nineteen times. At each mention, Pharaoh's resistance increases. Pharaoh himself initiates this process of growing disobedience (Ex. 8:15). He acts like a heavy drinker who deliberately plugs his ears against the advice of his friends. This is the initial stage of Pharaoh's disease—bringing it on himself. Then follows the second stage, where he can no longer help himself and where he must oppose God, just as an alcoholic must have another drink. At this latter stage, God's demands force Pharaoh ever deeper into the sin in which he has chosen to live. Only now do we read that the Lord hardens Pharaoh's heart (Ex. 9:12).

God, you might say, invades Pharaoh's disobedience to make missionary use of it. He compounds Pharaoh's hardness of heart for the purpose of offering the people of the world a display of his power. Without this hardening of Pharaoh's heart, God would not have set his people free with mighty signs. As we learn from Exodus 9:15, these signs are of great missionary value. Here God says to Pharaoh, "By now I could have stretched out my hand and struck you and your people with a plague that would have wiped you off the earth." This prompts the question: If God could have done that, why didn't he do it? The answer follows. "But I have raised you up for this very purpose, that I might show you my power and that my name might be proclaimed in all the earth."

Egypt's Gods Are Dethroned

God uses Pharaoh's disobedience for missionary purposes. How? By making it public knowledge through a series of mighty signs and wonders that the gods of Egypt do not keep their promises, as he does.

Snakes (Ex. 7:8-13). Why does God turn Aaron's rod into a snake? The answer relates to Egypt's geography. With the exception of a long, narrow strip of arable land on either side of the River Nile, Egypt consisted of nothing but desert region. In this region, so the Egyptians believed, no gods resided. Only snakes, dangerous snakes. By having Aaron's rod swallow up the rods of the Egyptian magicians, God demonstrates that he has power where Egypt's gods do not: over the desert.

Blood (Ex. 7:14-24). Why does God turn the water of the Nile into blood? The answer relates to Egypt's agriculture. Egyptian agriculture depended on the annual flooding of the Nile. Unless this flooding took place, the arable strip of land along both banks as well as the entire delta area remained dry and unproductive. Overseeing this annual rising of the Nile water was the god Hapi. By turning Nile water into blood, God demonstrates his superiority over Hapi. Significantly, Exodus 7:25 claims that God, not Moses, struck the Nile. God, not Moses, defeated Hapi. When the water turned red, "Pharaoh 'saw' the blood of his god now slain by the living God of Israel" (Knight, *Narration,* p. 59).

Frogs (Ex. 8:1-15). Why does God make the Nile swarm with frogs? Each year, Egypt experienced a frog season when, all along the banks of the Nile, people were forced, night after night, to listen to a cacophony of croaking frogs. The god in charge of regulating this annual affliction was Hekht. This female deity "protected the crocodiles in the river; these were the enemies of the frogs. On the other hand a plague of frogs means a promising rise in the level of the Nile. So Hekht was also regarded as the symbol of fertility" (Knight, *Narration,* p. 62). With unheard-of numbers of frogs overrunning the country, things clearly have gotten out of Hekht's hand. Once more, Yahweh has proven himself mightier than Egypt's gods.

Livestock (Ex. 9:1-7). Why does God send a terrible disease on Egypt's livestock? God sends this because it represents a blow at such local deities as the calf of Ur-Mer and the bull Bakis.

Darkness (Ex. 10:21-29). Why does God send a thick darkness over the land of Egypt, "darkness that can be felt"? This plague reveals God's "battle against Amen-Ra, the sun-god, the source of all life, whom even Pharaoh worshiped as his divine father" (Knight, *Narration,* p. 79). The eclipse of the sun means the eclipse of Amen-Ra.

What result does the defeat of some of Egypt's gods have? Exodus 9:18 offers one answer to this question. Tomorrow, God tells Pharaoh, I will send the worst hailstorm (this is God's word of judgment!). Therefore (and now follows God's word of grace!), get your livestock and everything you have to a place of shelter.

Because of this word of judgment and grace, a division takes place among the Egyptians. Some believe what God says; others do not. Those who believe God's word put their livestock under shelter. Even some of Pharaoh's servants "feared the word of the LORD" (Ex. 9:20). They feared it before the hail came down. Pagan people hear and obey the word of God. But this would never have happened if God had not first hardened Pharaoh's heart. God not only is merciful to the Hebrews, he also shows mercy to the Egyptians as a preview of the day when Egypt will be united with Israel as equal members of the chosen people. "In that day Israel will be the third, along with Egypt and Assyria, a blessing on the earth. The LORD Almighty will bless them, saying, 'Blessed be Egypt my people, Assyria my handiwork, and Israel my inheritance' " (Isa. 19:24f.).

God Binds Himself to Israel

Why to Israel?

Why did God choose Israel to carry out his mission to the peoples of the world? Why didn't he, instead, choose the Egyptians with their scholarship? Or the Babylonians with their wisdom? Or, centuries later, the Greeks with their philosophy and science? Or the Romans with their genius for law and order? It would seem that under any of these choices God's mission in the world would have fared better and been expedited more efficiently. Why did God choose Israel to be "a kingdom of priests and a holy nation" (Ex. 19:6), to stand before him on behalf of all the people of the world?

One reason is that there are definite advantages to such a choice. It allows God to mold Israel like a lump of unformed clay and to build it into a nation that will not be constantly tempted to look back to its "glorious past" and its "honored traditions."

A much more important reason is that such a choice is in harmony with the mystery surrounding the name "I AM WHO I AM." This name means that God's ways are always higher than our ways and God's thoughts than our thoughts. It is God's nature to go against the human grain; to choose what is foolish in the world, to shame the wise; to choose what is weak in the world, to shame the strong; to choose what is low and despised in the world, so that no human being may boast in his presence (1 Cor. 1:27f.). To bless the world, God chose a people who are not a people.

After escaping destruction at the Red Sea, the people of Israel sing this song to the LORD: "I will sing to the Lord, for he is highly exalted. The horse and its rider he has hurled into the sea" (Ex. 15:1). They confess that the rescue is due to an act of God. They confess this, not just because they believe that God has acted on their behalf, or because they have the conviction or the feeling that God has redeemed them. Rather, Israel confesses that God brought them out of Egypt because God had previously promised to do so. Israel experiences the Red Sea deliverance as the fulfillment of a divine promise. This deliverance began when, from the burning bush, God said to Moses, "I have indeed seen the misery of my people. . . . so I have come down to rescue them from the hand of the Egyptians" (Ex. 3:7f.). What prompted God to rescue Israel was not a momentary impulse—one that could conceivably be reversed later, on a new impulse. Rather, God acted redemptively in order to fulfill his previously made promise, not just at the Red Sea, but throughout the history of his servant people. He acted in the same way, for example, when they first broke the covenant by worshiping a golden calf. I will destroy this stiff-necked people, God says to Moses. How does Moses stem this outburst of divine wrath? As the true mediator between God and his people, Moses softens God's anger by reminding him of his past promises. "Remember your servants Abraham, Isaac, and Israel, to whom you swore by your own self: 'I will make your descendants as numerous as the stars in the sky and I will give your descendants all this land I promised them, and it will be their inheritance forever' " (Ex. 32:13). Having been reminded of these promises, God repents of his intention to do away with Israel.

The Covenant

The foundation stone of the new life to which God calls the liberated Hebrew slaves is the covenant. God tells them: "You yourselves have seen what I did to Egypt, and how I carried you on eagles' wings and brought you to myself. Now if you obey me fully and keep my covenant, then out of all nations you will be my treasured possession" (Ex. 19:4f.). God binds himself to these people by way of a covenant. What does this mean?

A means of survival. In the ancient Near East, covenants were frequently a means of survival. Behind the practice of making covenants stood the ugly reality of a "dog eats dog" world, of rival tribes and nations and empires that were constantly at each other's throat. The threat of defeat and annihilation were constantly felt. Hence the feverish efforts of chieftains and kings to make covenants with each other.

The Old Testament uses this principle of the covenant to describe the relation between God and his servant people. God takes Israel under his protection. He binds Israel to himself by means of a covenant, as otherwise it would not survive.

Two kinds. In the ancient Near East there existed two kinds of covenant. One was an agreement between equal partners, as when two tribes pledged themselves to mutual military assistance, or as in the covenant between David and Jonathan (1 Sam. 20). The other kind was the so-called royal covenant. Here there was no equality. The ruler concluded a covenant, not *with* his subjects, but *for* them. One partner was lord; the other partner was servant.

It is this kind of covenant that God makes with Israel. The initiative belongs wholly to God. "I carried you on eagles' wings and brought you to myself" (Ex. 19:4). God's relationship with Israel is like that of an eagle "who stirs up his nest and hovers hither and thither above it in order to teach his young how to fly. . . . The great eagle spreads out his wings over the nestlings; he takes up one of them, a shy or weary one, and bears it upon his pinions; until it can at length dare the flight itself and follows the father in his mounting gyrations. Here we have election, deliverance and education; all in one" (Martin Buber, *Moses*, p. 102).

The Sinaitic covenant (Ex. 19-24). Although the deliverance from Egypt may dominate the book of Exodus, it is only introductory. The goal of the Exodus is Mount Sinai. Here God concludes a royal covenant between himself and Israel. Here God spells out the terms under which he binds himself to Israel.

The basis of all that God requires of Israel is the Ten Commandments (Ex. 20:2-17). The many and various laws that follow in Exodus, Leviticus, Numbers, and Deuteronomy are concrete applications of the Ten Commandments to the particular circumstances of the times. Together, these laws mark the boundary beyond which Israel cannot trespass without breaking the covenant.

The great number and variety of these laws may be rather confusing. When you read them, keep three things in mind.

First, these laws bear on every aspect of life. In their totality and variety they remind us that there is no area, either public or private, over which God's rule does not extend. To read these laws is to become aware that God lays claim to the entire person. This total claim is most impressively set forth in Deuteronomy 27:15-25: "Cursed is the man who carves an image or casts an idol . . . and sets it up in secret. . . . Cursed is the man who dishonors his father or his mother. . . . who moves his neighbor's boundary stone. . . . who leads the blind astray on the road. . . . who withholds justice from the alien, the fatherless or the widow. . . . who sleeps with his father's wife. . . . with any animal . . . with his sister. . . . with his mother-in-law. . . . who kills his neighbor secretly. . . . who accepts a bribe to kill an innocent person."

All these prohibitions have one thing in common. They deal with sin committed in secret. "There are many areas of life which the arm of earthly law and justice is too short to reach, or with which perhaps such law is incompetent to deal. But none of these areas escapes the watchful eyes of God, and the people are called to recognize that he exercises his righteous judgment even over that which is hidden from the eyes of men" (Gerhard von Rad, *Moses*, p. 57f.).

Second, many of these laws invite God's people to exercise compassion. They show sympathy and consideration for the weak and defenseless. They secure the rights of servants, slaves, captives, widows, orphans, sojourners, the maimed, the poor. A good example is the law against keeping overnight the cloak taken as security. "Return his cloak to him by sunset so that he may sleep in it. Then he will thank you" (Deut. 24:13f.). Another example is the law on gleaning. "When you are harvesting in your field and you overlook a sheaf, do not go back to get it. Leave it for the alien, the fatherless and the widow" (Deut. 24:19). This spirit of compassion extends even to animals, so that an ox treading out the grain could not be muzzled (Deut. 25:4), or a kid be boiled in its mother's milk (Ex. 23:19).

Third, when reading these many and various laws, keep in mind that they should never be cut from their foundation in God's saving action. Israel is called to keep these laws out of gratitude for God's unmerited grace displayed in the Exodus. The fundamental sin of Israel is not breaking this or that law, but showing no gratitude. Why must Israel have mercy on strangers? Not for mercy's sake, nor alone because God, by nature, is merciful. Above all, it must be merciful because Israel itself at one time was a stranger befriended and redeemed by God. "Do not mistreat an alien or oppress him, for you were aliens in Egypt" (Ex. 22:21). God's covenant law "is for the most part law conceived out of the experienced reality of a merciful God, who himself took a victimized nation from among the society of nations and treated it with unparalleled and undeserved gentleness and mercy" (Napier, *From Faith to Faith*, p. 202). The Israelites are to obey God, not as slaves, but as people who remember in gratitude the gracious deeds of their liberator.

Two: God Names Himself

Chapter Review Questions

1. Why were the Israelites so interested in knowing God's precise name?

2. By what name does God reveal himself to Moses?

3. Where does the name "I AM" occur in the New Testament?

4. How does God establish his supremacy over the gods of Egypt?

5. What kind of covenant does God enter into with Israel?

6. Which three things must we keep in mind when reading the many and various laws in the books of Exodus, Leviticus, Numbers, and Deuteronomy?

General Discussion Questions

1. What does the story of God's call of Moses tell us about our own call?

2. In striking contrast to the rest of the book of Exodus, the first two chapters tell us nothing about what God is doing. God is mentioned in every chapter except 37-39. Furthermore, God speaks in every other chapter except 18 and 35-39. This God, so active and vocal in the rest of the book, is unobtrusive and silent in the events of chapters 1-2. What do you think accounts for this silence?

3. What kind of miracle took place at the Red Sea?

4. Why do you think God selects the wilderness as the cradle of Israel's birth?

5. Exodus 16 tells the story of how the people grumbled about the lack of food in the desert, and how God responded to their complaints by providing manna. Why do you think the manna fell daily? Why not weekly?

6. In what ways is the Exodus like Easter?

Notes

Three: God Brings
His People Home

The Book of Joshua

Was it God's will that the Israelites should invade a country already occupied by other people? Were the Israelites right in thinking that God wanted them to butcher the people who were already there and to put their cities to the torch?

These questions have often been asked. What is the answer? Is it that the Israelites were as barbarous in some way, as all the other people of that time? Is it that they were land-hungry nomads whose behavior did not rise significantly above the barbarism of their age? This kind of answer does not address the heart of the matter. The key lies elsewhere. It lies in seeing a clear line of divine purpose from the days of Abraham through the settlement in Palestine and on into the future. Let us trace that line.

The Promised Land

A down payment. There probably is no more persistent theme in the first six books of the Bible than that of land promised and later granted by God. The promise of land is first made in Genesis 12:1, "Go to the land I will show you." It is repeated thirteen times in Genesis, five times in Exodus, three times in Numbers, fifteen times in Deuteronomy, and twice in Joshua.

The patriarchs are the first ones to receive the promise of the land. Though they already live in it, it remains a land in which they are still sojourners. Abraham, for example, does not own a square yard of it. Only after his wife, Sarah, dies, and after paying an exorbitant price, does he become the owner of a small piece of promised land. "So Ephron's field in Machpelah near Mamre—both the field and the cave in it, and all the trees within the borders of the field—was deeded to Abraham as his property" (Gen. 23:17f.).

This field with the cave is the down payment on the promised land. In this cave Abraham and Sarah, Isaac and Rebekah, and Jacob and Leah are buried. Only in death do they cease to be sojourners in Canaanite territory and enter a piece of the promised land that is legally theirs. This cave is the meeting place for those who have been promised the land but have never possessed it. Here they meet and wait for God to make true his promise to them.

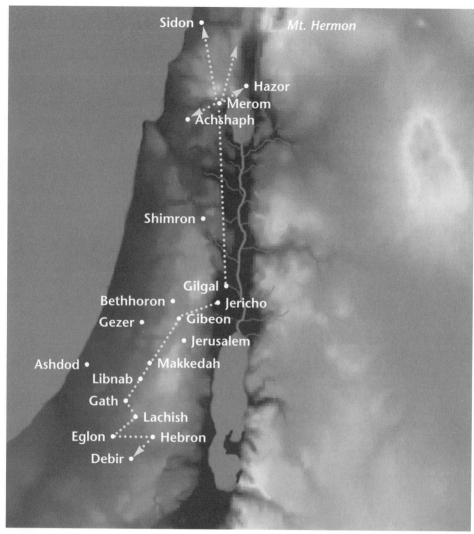

Joshua's Military Campaigns

The time of Joshua is the time of fulfillment. Israel takes possession of the land and divides it among its twelve tribes.

A heritage. Palestine never did belong to the Canaanites. God had been the rightful owner of it all along. Now, with the conquest, God takes it away from the Canaanites and gives it to the Israelites, but on a provisional basis, for God remains the owner of it. God tells Israel, "The land must not be sold permanently, because the land is mine" (Lev. 25:23). The land, like Israel itself, ever resides under God's jurisdiction. Both Israel and the land must always respond to God's bidding. Both must respond with obedience to his will. "The productivity of the land is determined by the conduct of those who inhabit it, for both land and people live under a common historical and moral sovereignty. When God commands it to yield, the land breaks forth into

38

fertility and abundance; when he pronounces judgment upon it, it lies barren and desolate, and all that it has to yield is thorns and thistles" (James Muilenburg, *The Way of Israel*, p. 85f.).

The Conquest

The book of Joshua provides us with the main account of the conquest. The Israelites cross the Jordan River and capture the cities of Jericho and Ai. Then, in quick succession, they carry out three successful military operations. First, they penetrate to the center of the land (Josh. 7-9); next, an alliance of five Canaanite kings from the south is defeated and the whole of southern Palestine occupied (Josh. 10); finally, the northern Canaanite kings are defeated and their cities fall into Israelite hands (Josh. 11). The outcome is that the mountainous area of Palestine is now largely Israelite territory. If it hadn't been for the chariots of iron (Judg. 1:19), the plains along the coast of the Mediterranean would have been conquered as well.

After the land has been conquered, the individual tribes are allotted portions of it (Josh. 13-21).

Besides the book of Joshua, the opening chapter of Judges also provides us with an account of the conquest. This chapter makes it plain that the conquest was not as quick and complete a process as a casual reading of the book of Joshua might lead one to suppose. Judges 1 shows how long a process—and how far from complete—Israelite occupation of Palestine really was. The conquest is by no means the story of one success after another; it suffers many setbacks. Since Israel fights on foot, it cannot venture down onto the plains to fight the chariots of the city-states there (Josh. 17:16; Judg. 1:19). This prevents Israel from occupying the plains. Only once do Israelite soldiers take on a contingent of chariots, when Deborah and Barak order them to attack a Canaanite army of nine hundred chariots on the Plain of Esdraelon below. From a military point of view, it is a suicide mission. But as the Israelites pour down the hills, so does the rain. "The torrent Kishon swept [the Canaanite army] away, the onrushing torrent, the torrent Kishon" (Judg. 5:21, NRSV). The plain turns into a sea, the chariots bog down, and Israel is victorious.

Despite this local victory, the plains remain unconquered; so do a great many Canaanite cities and villages (Judg. 1:27-33). The occupation of Palestine, therefore, is both slow and partial and continues at least until David consolidates the entire land. Not until that time does Palestine become the home of Israel.

Openness to a Future

When the Israelites have settled in Palestine, is the promise of land fulfilled? Only partially. The promise of land remains open to a future fulfillment. In fact, so do all of God's promises in the Old Testament, for the simple reason that the ultimate fulfillment of Israel's history lies beyond the horizon of the Old Testament. Israel's existence is always preliminary to what is still to come. Israel is always on pilgrimage, even when "settled." God's command is

Slavery in Egypt ◄   ► Conquest of Canaan begins

► Rule of Judges begins

• Exodus

• Death of Moses;
Joshua enters promised land

perpetually in force: "The poles are to remain in the rings of this ark; they are not to be removed" (Ex. 25:15). Israel must always be prepared to move on.

Although the conquest under Joshua is the historical fulfillment of the promise first made to Abraham, the Old Testament never regards the conquest to be its full and final fulfillment. When the conquest is first made, it is said that everything promised has been fulfilled. "So the LORD gave Israel all the land he had sworn to give their forefathers and they took possession of it and settled there. . . . Not one of all the LORD's good promises to the house of Israel failed; every one was fulfilled" (Josh. 21:43-45). But already five chapters later, in Judges 2, the sacred writer feels obliged to record a jarring note—the fact that Israel is forced to share this land with the Canaanites. "The LORD had allowed those nations to remain; he did not drive them out at once by giving them into the hands of Joshua" (Judg. 2:23).

The promise of land, therefore, remains in effect. Never is there any satisfactory historical fulfillment of it. Never does Israel come to the rest which God has promised (Deut. 12:9ff.; 25:19). Throughout the history of Israel the promise remains open to a future fulfillment, so that the letter to the Hebrews can take it up again and, in the light of Jesus' resurrection, reveal new depths of meaning. "Therefore, since the promise of entering his rest still stands, let us be careful that none of you be found to have fallen short of it" (Heb. 4:1).

The Book of Judges

The Theme

The book of Judges can be summarized in a simple sentence: God's power is made perfect in human weakness. This one theme can be said to unite all the different stories. The book of Judges is not a series of heroic tales. Its only hero is God, who works his victories through the weakness of the judges. This is most clearly illustrated by the story of Gideon's war against the Midianites. Why does God tell Gideon to reduce his army to three hundred men (Judg. 7:8)? To show that he, not Gideon, delivers Midian into the hands of Israel.

The stories of the judges show a certain pattern. First the judge responds to a call from God. Then he publicly demonstrates his leadership talent by scoring a victory over the enemy. But from then on the line curves downward.

• Gideon

    • Birth of Samuel

      • Jephthah

       • Samson

Gideon, for example, requests of the Israelites who want him to rule over them that they give him the golden earrings of their spoil. Of these Gideon makes an "ephod" and puts it in his city, where it becomes the center of Baal worship. "All Israel prostituted themselves by worshiping it there, and it became a snare to Gideon and to his family" (Judg. 8:27).

Jephthah, after defeating the Ammonites, offers his own daughter as a sacrifice to God because he had vowed to offer "whatever comes out of the door of my house to meet me when I return in triumph from the Ammonites" (Judg. 11:31). Furthermore, after his victory over the Ammonites, Jephthah is unable, or unwilling, to stop a bloody infight between two Israelite tribes— the Ephraimites from the west Jordan mountains and the Gileadites from the east Jordan region (Judg. 12:1-7). The hostility becomes so focused that a single word is made to decide whether people will live or die. This is how the book of Judges tells the story:

> The Gileadites captured the fords of the Jordan leading to Ephraim, and whenever a survivor of Ephraim said, "Let me cross over," the men of Gilead asked him, "Are you an Ephraimite?" If he replied, "No," they said, "All right, say 'Shibboleth.' " If he said, "Sibboleth," because he could not pronounce the word correctly, they seized him and killed him at the fords of the Jordan. Forty-two thousand Ephraimites were killed at that time (Judg. 12:5f.).

It is significant that the meaning of the word *shibboleth* in this context is not at all clear; nor does its meaning matter. "We are not dealing with a confession of some kind, the content of which was decisive, but simply with a completely empty word on which life and death were made to depend" (Gerhard von Rad, *God at Work in Israel,* p. 41). It is also significant that the report of this internal quarrel is followed immediately by the telling words that this took place while Jephthah was judge. "Jephthah led Israel six years. Then Jephthah the Gileadite died, and was buried in a town in Gilead" (Judg. 12:7).

In the story of Samson, too, the line curves downward. Samson increasingly squanders his God-given power in the great conflict between eros (human love) and calling (divine task). More and more he plays with his charisma.

A pessimism pervades all these stories. Only for a little while are men like Gideon, Jephthah, and Samson able, thanks to their God-given charisma, to rise above their limitations. Behind all of these stories there lies this unspoken question: If not Gideon, or Jephthah, or Samson, who? Where is the one who will deliver God's people, not merely once or twice, but for all time to come?

Charismatic Leadership

The Israel of post-conquest days is not at all a nation as we understand that word today. On the contrary, it is a loose federation of twelve tribes united in covenant with God. This covenant both creates its society and holds it together. Israel has no statehood, no centralized government, no capital city. Its various tribes are independent political units whose religious focal point is a portable tent-shrine that houses the ark of the covenant—the throne of the invisible God. This shrine, which initially traveled from tribe to tribe, eventually finds a permanent resting place in Shiloh (1 Sam. 1-4). There the tribal people gather on feast days to seek the presence of God and renew their covenant allegiance to him.

This form of political organization is able to survive only as long as the tribes are relatively small and cohesive. Outside danger is dealt with by a judge, a person upon whom God pours out his Spirit (Judg. 3:10), and who then calls out the neighboring tribes and repels the enemy. However, after the enemy has been defeated, the victory is not followed up. No attempts are made to besiege and capture enemy cities. It is sufficient that the enemy has been repelled. After the victory the quickly organized Israelite army disbands and the leader retires. For he is not a king. He returns to his father's house, to his cattle, to his land. He is again what he was before: an ordinary tribesman.

Judges 2:13-18 summarily describes the period of the judges. It lists the four acts of the recurring drama.

Act 1: Israel forsakes the Lord and serves the Baals.

Act 2: The anger of the Lord is kindled against Israel, and he gives them over to raiders.

Act 3: The people groan because of those who afflict and oppress them.

Act 4: The Lord is moved to compassion and raises up a judge who saves them from the power of the oppressor.

After the judge dies, the same drama begins to repeat itself. The people turn back and behave as before, "following other gods and serving and worshiping them" (Judg. 2:19).

For some two hundred years following the conquest, the Israelite tribes live under this arrangement. The focal point of its tribal confederation remains the charismatic leader. Israel does not imitate the city-state model of the Canaanites; nor does it organize a political state. It continues to reject the idea of a monarchy. When the Israelites ask Gideon and his descendants to rule over them, Gideon answers: "I will not rule over you, nor will my son rule over you. The LORD will rule over" (Judg. 8:23). Jotham, too, opposes monarchical rule. In his well-known fable of the trees (Judg. 9:7-21) he lets it be known that only a good-for-nothing thornbush of a person would consider being king over Israel.

The Philistines

Matters would have remained unchanged had not the Philistines put the charismatic leadership to a severe test. The Israelite league of tribes, humanly speaking, had been able to survive this long because its enemies had been small and fragmented. It had never been challenged by a strong, well-organized state. The Philistines were precisely that. Having been driven from their homes by Greek invaders, they had come from across the sea to Palestine.

They had failed in an attempt to enter Egypt but in the twelfth century before Christ had established themselves along the sea-coast of Palestine. They proved to be the sort of enemy with which Israel's loose federation could not cope. "Unlike previous foes, the Philistines did not pose a limited threat that concerned only adjacent tribes, nor one that the tribal rally could deal with at a blow; aiming at conquest, they threatened Israel in her totality and with her life. They were, moreover, disciplined soldiers whose weapons, owing especially to their monopoly on iron, were superior. . . . The ill-trained, ill-equipped Israelite tribal levies could stand little chance against such a foe in open battle" (John Bright, *A History of Israel,* p. 164).

The decisive battle between Israel and Philistia is recorded in 1 Samuel 4. The ark of the covenant is captured. Israel is utterly defeated. Its war potential is destroyed by its being forbidden to work in metal. "Not a blacksmith could be found in the whole land of Israel, because the Philistines had said, 'Otherwise the Hebrews will make swords or spears!' " (1 Sam. 13:19).

In the face of this emergency, the first step towards statehood is made. For a freeborn Israelite the choice is clear: take that step or be enslaved. Yet it is a difficult choice, for it represents a step toward an authority that is foreign to Israel's tradition. We will study this in the next chapter.

Worship of the Baals

Before he died, Joshua recognized the danger that his people would be Canaanized. He called them together to Shechem and made them promise that they would remain faithful to their covenant with Yahweh (Josh. 24). But the promise is not kept. Most of the second generation of settlers forsake Yahweh and serve the Baals instead (Judg. 2:10f.; 3:7). Gideon does indeed destroy the altar of Baal belonging to his father and builds an altar to Yahweh instead, but soon after his death the people of Israel "again prostituted themselves to the Baals" (Judg. 8:33). Why so soon? What is the particular attraction of Baal worship?

When Israel invades Palestine, it is a nomadic people. When it conquers Canaanite land, it changes over to agriculture and, in the process, to Canaanite life and worship. For the two are related. In changing over to agriculture, Israel is immediately confronted by a fact that it has never   43 seriously included in its religious life: the fertility of the soil. Israel knows God as a nomadic God, who traveled through the wilderness before his people. But is he also the God of the soil, of seed and harvest, of conception and fertility? This question gives birth to the great crisis that occurs in Israel's religious life after it enters Palestine. Is the God of the Exodus also the God of fertility? Are not the Baals—the local Canaanite deities—lord of the land?

In ancient times, tillable soil was deeply sacred. The soil, it was held, harbored a divine mystery. A farmer could not simply till it. To do so, he needed divine permission and guidance. In Canaan, the Baals provided both. The Canaanites believed that the mystery of fertility was hidden in the depth of the ground. There male and female powers, Baal (lord) and Baalath (lady) copulated—countless pairs of them. This divine sexual activity rendered the soil fruitful.

Of this divine activity people were not merely passive witnesses. By an act of "sacred" pairing, in which man and woman imitated Baal and Baalath, they were able to participate and so increase the fertility of the soil. The "sacred" prostitute, therefore, was prominent in the Canaanite Baal cult. She, sometimes he, provided sex not so much for money and pleasure but for religious reasons, to establish contact with the forces of reproduction within the soil. Baal worship, by nature, was orgiastic.

This being the case, it is easy to see why Israel from the outset fell under the spell of Baal worship. A Canaanite farmer could get in touch with the divine forces in this plot of land by getting in touch with his sexual desires. To establish contact with the Baals, he needed only to follow physical desires.

By worshiping the Baals, Israel did not mean to depart from Yahweh; in times of crisis the people did turn to him. But in agricultural matters they turned to the Baals. They thanked Yahweh for military victories and the Baals for the good gifts of the land. "When the enemy oppressed, they had only to throw down the altars of the local *baalim* (Judg. 6:28), and thereby the requirements of the hour were accomplished. As soon as the war of liberation is proclaimed, there is in reality none but YHVH, and immediately the *baalim* are forgotten, . . . But when peace returns and the regular life of soil-cultivation is re-established, it is difficult for YHVH to stand up against the small nameless powers, swarming everywhere without special forms. He, YHVH, cannot remain really the Lord of the people, the God of Israel in the old absolute sense, unless He brings under his rule the domain of the new, agricultural form of life" (Martin Buber, *The Prophetic Faith*, p. 74f.).

Yahweh and the Baals are complete opposites. The Baals never summon people beyond their animal nature. Rather, they foster that animal nature, for they pose no moral standards. Yahweh, on the other hand, can be worshiped only when he is obeyed. Worship of Yahweh apart from moral response is nothing more than a pagan response.

The most fundamental choice Israel is asked to make during its history is the choice between Yahweh and the Baals. Repeatedly it is confronted with the question: "How long will you waver between two opinions? If the LORD is God, follow him; but if Baal is God, then follow him" (1 Kings 18:21). Had Israel followed Baal, it would have ceased to be God's people, and its heritage would not have reached us.

Three: God Brings His People Home

Chapter Review Questions

1. The book of Joshua records the story of Israel's annihilation of the Canaanites. Time after time, Joshua encourages the Israelites to pursue their enemies, "for the Lord has given them into your hand." Was this destruction necessary? Was it God's will?

2. In brief outline, describe the Israelite conquest of Canaan.

3. According to Exodus 25:15, the poles were to remain in the rings of the ark. What does this signify?

4. What is the central question that lies behind the book of Judges?

5. Why is Baal worship so attractive?

General Discussion Questions

1. Read Joshua 4:1-7. What is the significance of the twelve stones? What helps us today to remember God's mighty acts?

2. What are the Baals of our day?

3. Read the story of Samson (Judg. 13-16). Why do you think Samson's picture is hanging in the Hebrews 11 "Hall of Faith"?

Notes

Four: God Chooses a King for His People

The books of Samuel and Kings narrate a continuous story that covers approximately five hundred years of Israelite history. If it were to be published separately in modern book form, this story would make a volume of about three hundred pages. Its title, as someone has suggested, might very well be *The Rise and Fall of the Hebrew Kingdom*.

The People Want a King

After Israel passes safely through the Red Sea, it accepts and confesses Yahweh as its king: "The LORD will reign for ever and ever" (Ex. 15:18). At Mount Sinai, Yahweh enters upon his kingly rule over Israel: "This is what you are to say to . . . the people of Israel: . . . you will be for me a kingdom of priests" (Ex. 19:3ff.).

The rise of kingship in Israel, therefore, poses a profound theological problem. How can a nation request a king if it already recognizes Yahweh as its exclusive king? Because of this problem, it is not surprising that kingship in Israel prevails only after a bitter struggle.

Under the leadership of Samuel, the last of the judges, Israel gathers sufficient strength to fight off the Philistines. But as Samuel grows older, people fear what may happen after he dies. Moreover, they see what power other nations have when they unify under the leadership of a king. They desire similar power for themselves. So they go to Samuel and make the following request: "Appoint a king to lead us, such as all the other nations have" (1 Sam. 8:5).

At first Samuel will not hear of it. The request runs counter to his deepest convictions. But God commands him to give in to the people's request: "It is not you they have rejected, but they have rejected me as their king" (1 Sam. 8:7). Samuel conveys this divine response to the people but at the same time warns them of what they may lose by having a king. A king's army, he points out, will take many of your sons. A king's palace will need many of your daughters. And the money to pay for all these things will come from the high taxes that you will be paying.

God wants the Israelites to realize the serious consequences of their request. Nevertheless, he grants it. More than that, he uses it for his own purposes. He establishes the Davidic dynasty from which, in the fullness of time, the savior king of the world will come.

Because so much controversy and tension surrounded the rise of the Hebrew kingdom, one is able to hear two different voices in the account of the origin of kingship—that of the monarchists and that of the anti-monarchists. The monarchists accept the kingship as a gift of God. The anti-monarchists are very critical of the kingship.

Both voices, the one favoring and the one opposing the kingship, together reflect the total situation at the time when the monarchy came into being. Yes, "the kingship *was* God's gift at a difficult period; the anointing of the king was at God's command and therefore the monarchy had God's promise; *but* at the same time this gift of kingship was fraught with dangers and temptations from the very beginning. The hostile part in the account of the origin of kingship corresponds to the final judgment on the monarchy: namely, that it was largely to blame for turning Israel aside to disobedience" (Claus Westermann, *A Thousand Years and a Day*, p. 113).

The figure of Samuel can be understood only in the light of this tension surrounding the rise of kingship. Samuel is first displeased with the people's request for a king (1 Sam. 8). Then he appears as Saul's patron (1 Sam. 9-10). Finally, when Saul gets out of hand, he deserts him and breaks with him (1 Sam. 13:8-15; 15).

The Opening Trio

Israel's request for a king, God says (1 Sam. 8:7), is a rejection of him as king over Israel. It represents a "fall" from Israel's ancient profession of Yahweh's exclusive kingship, comparable in some ways to the fall of the first human parents. The earliest history of humankind as recorded in the early chapters of Genesis and the history of the Hebrew kingdom as recorded in the books of Samuel and Kings have some striking features in common. This is not surprising, for what is true of humanity as a whole must also be true of Israel's kings. Both histories open with an act of disobedience and rejection.

In the third chapter of his book *From Faith to Faith*, B. Davie Napier lists a number of these common features. We will incorporate them in the material below.

King Saul

The story of Saul is strikingly similar in structure to the story of the Garden of Eden in Genesis 2 and 3. This does not mean that the Saul story was modeled after the garden story. It means, rather, that Israel viewed both the history of humankind and its own history from a single perspective. It means that God does not operate with a double standard—one for humankind and one for his servant people. He judges all sin by a single standard. That being the case, parallel features are to be expected. Napier notes six of them.

1. As God places the man in the Garden of Eden, so he places Saul in the kingdom—both under the most favorable circumstances.

2. Both must meet one condition: obedience to God. To be the first man God says, "You must not eat from the tree of the knowledge of good and evil, for when you eat of it you will surely die" (Gen. 2:17). To Israel and Saul he says, "If both you and the king who reigns over you follow the LORD your God —good! but if you do not obey the LORD, and if you rebel against his commands, his hand will be against you, as it was against your fathers" (1 Sam. 12:14f.).

3. This one condition is violated in both cases, and for a similar reason—the reasonableness of the act of disobedience. Disobedience in the garden is rationalized in these words: "When the woman saw that the fruit of the tree was good for food and pleasing to the eye and also desirable for gaining wisdom, she took some and ate it. She also gave some to her husband, who was with her, and he ate it" (Gen. 3:6). Saul breaks the law of God by usurping the function of the priest; when Samuel is late in coming, Saul offers the customary sacrifice before the battle. To Samuel he explains his action as follows: "When I saw that the men were scattering, and that you did not come at the set time, and that the Philistines were assembling at Micmash . . . I felt compelled to offer the burnt offering" (1 Sam. 13:11f.).

4. In both cases an effort is made to put the blame on someone else. Adam says to God, "The woman you put here with me—she gave me some fruit from the tree, and I ate it" (Gen. 3:12). Saul, after disobeying God by sparing the better portions of the Amalekite flock, passes his guilt on to the soldiers: "I completely destroyed the Amalekites. . . . The soldiers took . . . plunder . . . to sacrifice to the LORD your God at Gilgal" (1 Sam. 15:20f.).

5. In both cases appropriate judgment is pronounced and executed after the condition of obedience has been violated. The judgment in either case is expulsion. The man is expelled from the Garden of Eden: "He must not be allowed to reach out his hand and take also from the tree of life and eat, and live forever" (Gen. 3:22). Saul is expelled from the kingship. "Because you have rejected the word of the LORD, he has rejected you as king" (1 Sam. 15:23).

6. In both stories, the fate of those who come after is sealed by the act of initial disobedience. As the first man's trespass leads to condemnation of all people, Saul's disobedience darkly foreshadows the ultimate fate of kingship in Israel. Writes Westermann: "Saul is like a rejected, condemned man, who suspects his fate but does not turn aside. Unyielding, he meets the Philistines in a last battle on Mount Gilboa. It is a terrible battle. Saul sees three of his sons fall. He himself is severely wounded by an arrow. In order not to be taken prisoner by the enemy he falls on his sword. His armor bearer dies with him. This dark and depressing picture of the first Israelite king has a symbolic significance. Israel's monarchy as a whole is

History of Iseral

1200BC	1100	1000	9C
		▶ United Kingdom	▶ Divided Kin
• Gideon			
		• Saul	• David	
		• Samuel	• Solomon	

depicted in Saul rather than in David. . . . The fate of the Israelite kingship has already been darkly hinted at in its first representative" (*Thousand Years*, p. 120).

King David

As the first book of Samuel closes, the Philistines have defeated the Israelites, and both Saul and three of his sons lie dead on the battlefield. The way is now open for David to become king.

The whole of 2 Samuel is devoted to the story of David as king. David greatly increases the power of the nation by unifying the northern and the southern tribes. He captures Jerusalem and makes it his capital. Then he brings the ark—the ancient national symbol of Yahweh's covenant with Israel—to Jerusalem. No decision has had greater consequences for this city. By the installation of the ark in Jerusalem, this city becomes more than the capital and the royal residence. It is elevated to a holy city, to God's dwelling place.

The bringing of the ark to Jerusalem is an occasion of great rejoicing. Psalm 24, in all probability, celebrates this occasion. As the festal procession advances toward the city gates, and the ark for the first time is carried into Jerusalem, the choir sings antiphonally:

Lift up your heads, O you gates;
lift them up, you ancient doors,
that the King of glory may come in.
Who is he, this King of glory?
The LORD Almighty—
he is the King of glory.
(v. 9-10)

Success, regrettably, goes to David's head. As his power increases, he begins to think that he can do whatever he pleases. Late one afternoon, when he gets up from his couch and walks upon the roof of his house, he sees Bathsheba, the wife of Uriah, and commits adultery with her. Bathsheba's husband, though a Hittite (2 Sam. 11:3), has taken a Yahweh name: Uri-Yah, meaning "Yahweh is light" or "Yahweh is my light." He is, therefore, David's brother "in Yahweh." In addition, he is deeply loyal to David as a soldier. His name appears on the honor roll of thirty-seven mighty men who served under David (2 Sam. 23:39).

52

► Exile of Israel   ► Exile of Judah

• Assyrian invasion of Israel • Babylonian invasion of Judah

God's verdict on David's sin is twofold. Not only has David sinned against his fellow humans, he also has sinned against God. Not only, says God, have you "struck down Uriah the Hittite with the sword and took his wife to be your own," but you also "despise the word of the Lord by doing what is evil in his eyes" (2 Sam. 12:9). God's punishment matches David's sin. His sin of killing Uriah is punished with corresponding violence: "the sword will never depart from your house." His sin of adultery is punished with corresponding tragedy within his own family: "Out of your own household I am going to bring calamity upon you" (2 Sam. 12:10f.).

If the story of Saul parallels the story of disobedience in the Garden of Eden, the story of David bears an interesting resemblance to the story of Cain and Abel in Genesis 4.

1. Neither in Cain's nor in David's case is there a valid external reason for the sin. Neither one acts under provocation. In both men, the urge to commit an act of violence emerges from within. From within, out of David's heart, came "evil thoughts . . . theft, murder, adultery, greed, malice, deceit" (Mark 7:21f.).

2. Both men commit an act of violence within their own community. Cain kills his brother and David sins against his loyal subjects.

3. Both men admit their guilt, Cain by implication (Gen. 4:13) and David openly: "I have sinned against the LORD" (2 Sam. 12:13).

4. Both receive a similar judgment. Cain is driven from the presence of God and becomes a fugitive and a wanderer on the earth (Gen. 4:12), and David is driven from Jerusalem and becomes a fugitive pursued by his own son (2 Sam. 15-18).

5. Both Cain and David are given the assurance that their lives will be protected. God puts a mark on Cain, "so that no one who found him would kill him" (Gen. 4:15), and says to David: "[I have] taken away your sin. You are not going to die" (2 Sam. 12:13).

King Solomon

In the later years of David's reign, intrigues and conspiracies develop around the question of who is to succeed David as king over Israel. Is it to be Prince Ammon, David's firstborn son and therefore heir apparent to the throne

(2 Sam. 3:2)? Or is Absalom to occupy the throne? Because Ammon raped Absalom's half-sister Tamar (2 Sam. 13), Absalom has Ammon murdered. With Ammon out of the way, Absalom is now the heir apparent. To accelerate the process of succession, Absalom conspires against his father, proclaims himself kin in Hebron, drives his father out of Jerusalem, but is subsequently killed by Joab, David's army commander. After Absalom's death it remains to be decided among David's surviving sons which of them shall succeed David. The eldest of them, Adonijah, has Joab the general and Abiathar the priest on his side. His rival, Solomon, too has powerful supporters—the priest Zadok, the prophet Nathan, Queen Bathsheba, and, last but not least, the royal bodyguard. In the end Solomon wins out.

As king, Solomon makes a promising beginning. He builds a magnificent temple and professes a humble faith. But soon he makes his nation rival other nations in the splendor of his court, the number of foreign princesses in his harem, the magnificence of his buildings, and the size of his army. As all of these can only be financed by higher and higher taxes, the inevitable result is estrangement between Solomon and his people. Without realizing it, he is destroying the unity of the nation. For example, to carry out his ambitious building program, Solomon raises a levy of forced labor out of all Israel, a levy that at one time numbered thirty thousand men (1 Kings 5:13). Since the North had four or five times the population of the South, we may safely assume that the bulk of the compulsory labor force came from the North. Evoking further resentment was Solomon's decision to divide his kingdom into twelve districts for the purpose of breaking down tribal loyalties and promoting national loyalty. By doing so, he stepped on sensitive tribal toes.

After Solomon's reign, the inevitable happens. The ten northern tribes break off and form a separate kingdom, Israel, while the southern part continues as the kingdom of Judah. Though the North's dissatisfaction predates Solomon, the ultimate blame for the split falls directly on Solomon (1 Kings 11:9, 11).

If the basic sin of Saul had been disobedience and that of David violence, Solomon's basic sin is apostasy. His foreign wives continue to worship the gods of their countries, and Solomon accommodates them by letting them build shrines for these goods. Eventually Solomon himself is drawn into these foreign cults and worships Ashtoreth, the goddess of the Sidonians, and Milcom, the abomination of the Ammonities (1 Kings 11:5).

Solomon's ambition for splendor and greatness and his apostasy from Yahweh result in the destruction of national unity, just as, in Genesis 11, the people's resolve to make a name for themselves had resulted in the confusion of language and the scattering abroad. As it was in the beginning, so it is under Solomon's reign. When people turn away from God to serve other gods, judgment and disunity are sure to follow.

The division of North and South was final. The two kingdoms never reunited. The division was also extremely traumatic. Two centuries later the prophet Isaiah still remembers the disruption of the Israelite community as an event of unparalleled tragedy, when he warns: "The LORD will bring on you . . . a time unlike any since Ephraim [the northern tribes] broke away from Judah" (Isa. 7:17).

Weighed in the Balances

It is easy to tell when the book of Kings was written. All you have to do is check where the story ends. As 2 Kings closes, the temple and all the houses of Jerusalem have been burnt (25:9), and the king, with a large number of his people, has been deported to Babylon. The last event mentioned is the freeing of Jehoiachin, king of Judah, from prison in Babylon. This took place in the year 561 B.C. It is clear therefore that the final writing of Kings was done in Babylonian exile not too long after 561 B.C.

An important question to ask at this point is: Why was it written? As the southern kingdom came to a tragic end (the northern kingdom already had come to an end more than a century earlier), it seemed as though Israel as a nation had come to extinction. The questions on everybody's mind were: Why? Why has God rejected us? Are we not God's chosen people? Where did we go wrong?

The book of Kings was written to answer these questions. Israelites who had been taught by the great prophets took up the challenge of these questions, poured over the available documents, and subjected the entire history of the Hebrew kingdom to careful and godly scrutiny. To this history they brought an ultimate criterion and, in the light of this criterion, weighed all of Judah's and Israel's kings in the balances.

The criterion was obedience to God's command in Deuteronomy 12:1-7. Had these kings recognized the temple in Jerusalem as the only legitimate place of worship, or, in disobedience to this command, had they sacrificed on the "high places" where worship was shot through with pagan elements?

The centrality of worship in Jerusalem had been commanded by God to purify all Israelite worship from the foreign elements that had crept into all the shrines throughout the land. "Destroy completely all the places . . . where the nations you are dispossessing worship their gods. . . . you are to seek the place the LORD your God will choose from among all your tribes to put his Name there for his dwelling. To that place you must go" (Deut. 12:2-5). The book of Kings brings the entire history of the Hebrew kingdom under the judgment of this command.

Measured against this criterion, all the kings of the northern kingdom are condemned out of hand, for they all walked in the sin of Jeroboam. When the northern tribes split off from the southern tribes and the Davidic throne, they also cut themselves off from the promises God had made to the house of David (2 Sam. 7:11-16). It was not just a political schism. It was also a religious schism. Jeroboam, the first northern king, in order to keep his subjects away from the temple in Jerusalem, erects two golden calves, one in Dan and the other in Bethel. "You have gone up to Jerusalem long enough," he tells his people. "Here are your gods, O Israel, who brought you up out of

Egypt" (1 Kings 12:28). That is Jeroboam's chief sin. And all his successors are guilty of the same sin. Therefore all northern kings are condemned.

After the division, the southern kingdom represents the true Israel. But its unfaithfulness is almost as great as that of the North. Only two Judean kings receive unqualified praise: Hezekiah and Josiah. Six are approved conditionally: Asa, Jehoshaphat, Joash, Amaziah, Azariah, and Jotham. All the rest are reproached for having done what was evil in the sight of Yahweh.

If, on the whole, Judah's kings are not much better than Israel's kings, what explains God's restraint with Judah? Samaria, the northern capital, had fallen to the Assyrians in 721 B.C. Jerusalem, the southern capital, would fall to the Babylonians in 587 B.C. What explains the 134 years of additional grace? The answer lies in God's promise to establish and uphold the David dynasty. The command made about King Abijam is typical: "His heart was not fully devoted to the LORD his God, as the heart of David his forefather had been. Nevertheless, for David's sake the LORD his God gave him a lamp in Jerusalem by raising up a son to succeed him and by making Jerusalem strong" (1 Kings 15:3f.). God's promise to David is the restraining force that runs through the entire history of Judah and wards off the long-deserved judgment.

God Promises a King

God's light shines in the darkness of the history of the Hebrew kingdom from the words Nathan addresses to King David:

> The Lord declares to you that the Lord himself will establish a house for you: When your days are over and you rest with your fathers, I will raise up your offspring to succeed you, who will come from your own body, and I will establish his kingdom. He is the one who will build a house for my Name, and I will establish the throne of his kingdom forever. I will be his father, and he will be my son. When he does wrong, I will punish him with the rod of men, with floggings inflicted by men. But my love will never be taken away from him, as I took it away from Saul, whom I removed before you. Your house and your kingdom will endure forever before me; your throne will be established forever (2 Sam. 7:11-16).

These words begin a new chapter in the history of God's people. In them God promises unconditionally to establish the Davidic house in perpetuity and elects the reigning Davidic king to be his adopted son.

This momentous promise is preceded by the account of David bringing the ark to Jerusalem and of Michal, his wife, taking offense at seeing David dance in front of the ark. As a direct result of her displeasure with David, "Michal daughter of Saul has no children to the day of her death" (2 Sam. 6:23). Nathan's prophecy that David's house will rule forever follows right after this announcement, to remind the reader that the heir to the throne cannot come from her, David's first wife.

God's promise to David is followed by the account of who is to succeed David. Saul's crippled son, Meribaal (2 Sam. 9:1-13)? Prince Ammon, David's firstborn son? Or Absalom? Or Solomon? Rivalries, intrigues, and conspiracies spring up among the princes of the blood. As the succession drama unfolds, it becomes increasingly clear that, though people propose how God's promise is best fulfilled, God disposes. And when the monarchy in Israel comes to an end and all prospects that God will fulfill his promise to David grow dim, even then God preserves the Davidic throne, until, in the fullness of time, Jesus ascends it. "Blessed is he who comes in the name of the Lord! Blessed is the coming kingdom of our father David! Hosanna in the highest!" (Mark 11:9f.).

Four: God Chooses a King for His People

Chapter Review Questions

1. What was wrong with Israel asking for a king?

2. What is the importance of the books of Samuel and Kings?

3. Why did judgment come to the southern kingdom so much later (134 years) than it came to the northern kingdom?

4. What gospel message is proclaimed in 2 Samuel 7?

General Discussion Questions

1. King Saul has often been called a tragic hero. But was he?

2. Why, in his moving lament over Saul in 2 Samuel 1:19-27, doesn't David even slightly refer to Saul's instances of disobedience? Why does he refrain from making any moral judgment about Saul's suicide? Does this seem dishonest to you?

3. Why did David bring the ark to Jerusalem?

4. Why wouldn't God allow David to build a temple (2 Sam. 7)?

5. What is unique about God's promise to David in 2 Samuel 7?

6. What point is made by the so-called "succession story" (2 Sam. 6-20; 1 Kings 1-2)?

7. Read 1 Kings 4:20-34 and Micah 4:4. In what ways is the Solomonic age a preview of the messianic age?

Notes

Five: God Pleads with His People

What Is a Prophet?

Old Testament prophets walk the city streets, scrutinize the conduct of judges, pay visits to the marketplace, and are outraged by what they see. They roar their indignation at businesspeople for maximizing their profits. They scream in anger at judges for accepting bribes. They scold shopkeepers for using dishonest scales. They rage as though society is going to hell.

Why? Why do prophets elevate everyday injustices to cosmic proportions? Why are they so hypersensitive to social ills? Because prophets are people who stand "in the council of the LORD" (Jer. 23:18). They are not just God's mouthpieces, lending only their tongue to God. As God's close councillors, they also feel God's heart and suffer God's pain and experience God's anger. Prophets don't just hear God's voice. They also feel God's heart.

Prophets are not humanitarians moved by the plight of the poor. They are not revolutionaries summoning the people to the barricades. They are not social reformers introducing a new morality. They rave because God raves when his covenant people play fast and loose with the covenant law. "Will you steal and murder, commit adultery and perjury, burn incense to Baal and follow other gods you have not known, and then come and stand before me in this house, which bears my Name, and say, 'We are safe'—safe to do all these detestable things?" (Jer. 7:9-10).

Covenant Revivalists

Prophets passionately plead with Israel to rededicate itself to Yahweh, the covenant God. They beg Israel to embrace anew its covenant with Yahweh. They invite Israel to reorganize its life solely around Yahweh. Outside the covenant with Yahweh, prophets warn, life goes to pieces. A broken covenant means a broken community. When covenant vows are broken, society disintegrates.

The prophets' indictment against their contemporaries can be formulated in these two sentences: "You have broken the covenant. Repent!" All the rest is commentary.

Prophets of Doom

800BC	700	600	500
	▶ Exile of Israel	▶ Exile of Judah	
	• Assyrian invasion of Israel	• Babylonian invasion of Judah	
• Amos		• Jeremiah	

Classical Prophets

Classical prophecy in Israel runs parallel to the history of Israel's kings. Though the Old Testament speaks of prophets both before and after this period, prophecy in the classical sense is confined to the period of the monarchy.

The first period of the classical prophets, approximately from 750 to 700 B.C., coincides with the height of Assyrian power. At this time Amos and Hosea are active in the northern kingdom, Isaiah and Micah in the southern kingdom. The second period of the classical prophets, approximately from 650 to 600 B.C., coincides with the collapse of Assyria and the rise of Babylonia. The two most important events of this period are the destruction of Assyria (612 B.C.) and the destruction of Judah and subsequent capture of Jerusalem (587 B.C.) by the Babylonians. Nahum, Habakkuk, and Zephaniah address the first event; Jeremiah and Ezekiel, the second. In this chapter we will study two of these classical prophets.

The Prophet Amos

In his two opening chapters Amos brilliantly executes a circling movement whose ultimate target is Israel. Cleverly Amos tells his audience what it wants to hear. He begins by attacking the enemies of Israel, naming them one by one and identifying the characteristic sin of each. He accuses Damascus of torture, Gaza and Tyre of slave trade, Edom of its relentless hatred of Israel, Ammon of barbarity toward pregnant women, and Moab of irreverence toward the dead. Having highlighted each nation's characteristic sin, Amos then announces God's judgment: God will send a fire and it shall devour your strongholds.

Having finished his circling tour of Israel's surrounding nations, Amos then makes a surprise move. When the circle around Israel is closed, when escape is impossible, Amos suddenly turns to Israel and says: You also are doomed! For your behavior is no different from that of the nations that surround you. And don't think there is an escape. Don't appeal to your election. Don't say: Because we are God's chosen people we're exempt from judgment. For why have you been chosen? To be a light to the Gentile nations. The fact is, your darkness is as deep as theirs. Therefore, you are not immune to God's wrath. "For three sins of Israel, even for four, I will not turn back my wrath. [You] sell the righteous for silver, and the needy for a pair of sandals. [You] trample on the heads of the poor as upon the dust of the ground and deny justice to the oppressed. Father and son use the same girl and so profane my holy name" (Amos 2:6-7).

When legal aid is denied to the poor, when young women are sexually abused, when society's marginal people are denied justice, God roars from Zion and thunders from Jerusalem (Amos 1:2). He is starved for the kind of justice spelled out in the ancient covenant law.

Back to the Covenant!

Amos's single goal is to reactivate Israel's covenant with Yahweh. He tells Israel: You have divorced the covenant from the social obligations built into it. Amos derives all his accusations against Israel from the ancient covenant law which states, for example, that the poor and the weak shall not be oppressed and that none shall be in great need: "Do not take advantage of a widow or an orphan. If you do and they cry out to me, I will certainly hear their cry. My anger will be aroused, and I will kill you with the sword; your wives will become widows and your children fatherless" (Ex. 22:22-24).

In Amos's day, this covenant demand has been forgotten. What prevails instead are exploitation of the dispossessed, corrupt business practices, and lust for profit. Compounding the situation is the alliance between government and business for the purpose of preserving this unjust order.

In every Israelite city, legal disputes are settled by the elders—the leading citizens of the place. They sit at the city gates where all community affairs are discussed. The members of these popular courts are under instruction from the ancient covenant law as found, for example, in Exodus 23:1-3, 6-8. They are not to accept bribes. They are to acquit the innocent and condemn the guilty. In Amos's day, however, this ancient covenant law demanding equal justice for all is ignored and laws are written that favor the rich and encourage the rich to exploit the poor.

No Favorite Nation

Widespread corruption in Israel's society leads Amos to reflect on the scope of the covenant. Is God interested only in Israel? Israel is no more to God, Amos concludes, than the Cushites or the Philistines or the Arameans. It is, in fact, in a far worse position than any of these three. For it is the sinful people, not the people who do not worship Yahweh, that will be destroyed. "'Are not you Israelites the same to me as the Cushites?' declares the LORD. 'Did I not bring Israel up from Egypt, the Philistines from Caphtor and the Arameans from Kir? Surely the eyes of the Sovereign LORD are on the sinful kingdom. I will destroy it from the face of the earth'" (Amos 9:7-8).

God has no favorites, Amos is saying. One people is as dear to him as another. But isn't the Exodus from Egypt conclusive proof that God loves Israel with an exclusive love? (Amos 2:10; 3:1). No, Amos retorts, for other nations had their exodus too. God did bring Israel up out of the land of Egypt, true. But God also brought the Philistines from Caphtor and the Arameans from Kir. God is the God of all nations, not of Israel only. God wishes to bless the whole world. To accomplish this, he assigned Israel a special role. Israel, however, deceives itself when it views this role as a position of special privilege with Yahweh.

The Day of Yahweh

The Israel of Amos's day faces the future with hope. It believes in the coming of the day of Yahweh when God will triumph over all his enemies and establish his rule in the world. On that day Israel will be saved, regardless of its conduct.

Amos, however, castigates those who look forward to the day of Yahweh: "Woe to you who long for the day of the LORD! Why do you long for the day of the LORD? That day will be darkness, not light" (Amos 5:18).

New Beginning

Is judgment God's final word to Israel? No, says Amos, for when the fire of judgment has done its work, God will make a new beginning. "In that day I will restore David's fallen tent. I will repair its broken places, restore its ruins, and build it as it used to be" (Amos 9:11).

God is not a God of harsh and unbending justice. If he had been, he might have repudiated his covenant with Israel long ago. Repeatedly God forgives, hoping that Israel will repent. Though his condemnation of Israel's infidelity is harsh, the gate of repentance remains open. When God shows Amos in a vision the imminent destruction of Israel, Amos can offer no valid reason why God should not destroy it. All he can do is appeal to God's mercy. "Sovereign LORD, forgive! How can Jacob survive? He is so small!" (Amos 7:2).

God's judgment is never final. There is always a dimension in God's dealing with his people where compassion prevails over justice, where mercy is a perpetual possibility.

The Prophet Jeremiah

A little more than a hundred years have passed since Amos uttered his prophecies and the northern kingdom was destroyed. Now the bell is about to be tolled again, this time for the southern kingdom, and by Jeremiah.

Mission Impossible

Jeremiah's mission is to announce the downfall of the southern kingdom, the destruction of Jerusalem, and the end of the rule of the Davidic dynasty. It is a mission that borders on the superhuman. It requires that he confront a nationalism fanned by the hope for political independence and proclaim that political disaster is the inevitable judgment of God upon the people for their disloyalty. Like the prophets before him, Jeremiah is unheeded and shunned. Despised and rejected by his people, he suffers intensely. Without wife or children to support him (16:1f.), suspicious of his own brothers and relatives (12:6), in trouble with the authorities, at odds with most people and renouncing their lifestyle, Jeremiah is stalked by loneliness. But God tells him, "Do not be afraid of them, for I am with you and will rescue you" (1:8).

Does that ease Jeremiah's pain? Not very much. In loneliness and despair he complains to God that his mission is impossible:

O LORD, you deceived me,
    and I was deceived;
you overpowered me,
    and prevailed.
I am ridiculed all day long;
    everyone mocks me.
Whenever I speak, I cry out
    proclaiming, "violence and destruction."
So the word of the LORD has brought me
    insult and reproach all day long.
If I say, "I will not mention him
    or speak any more in his name,"
his word is in my heart like a fire,
    a fire shut up in my bones.
I am weary of holding it in;
    indeed, I cannot (20:7-9).

No Neat Outline

The book of Jeremiah is difficult reading. There seems to be confusion in its arrangement. The book lacks a continuous story for the reader to follow. Nor is there a logical progression of thought that binds all the different parts into a coherent whole. This seeming lack of order arises from the fact that, like most of the prophetic books, the book of Jeremiah is a kind of anthology. Chronological order should therefore not be expected. Just because a certain passage occurs earlier in the book does not mean that it was written before the passages that follow. If there is a principle of arrangement at all, it would seem to be a topical one. But even that is not carried out consistently. Yet this very observation, writes John Bright, is the beginning of understanding. "The prophetic books are indeed not books . . . as we understand the term. Nor are they books in the sense that most of the New Testament writings . . . or, for that matter, various of the writings of the Old Testament . . . are books. They are, rather, collections of prophetic sayings and other materials which have a long and complex history of transmission behind them" (*Jeremiah*, LVI f.). A neat outline, therefore, is out of the question. All we can do is note the broad structure:

The words of Jeremiah to Israel: Jeremiah 1:24; 30-33
The words of Jeremiah to the nations: Jeremiah 25; 46-51
The account of Jeremiah's life: Jeremiah 26-29; 34-45
The laments of Jeremiah: occurring between Jeremiah 10 and 20

The Old Covenant

In Jeremiah 2:1-13 we are witnesses to a covenant lawsuit. Acting as a prosecuting attorney representing Yahweh, Jeremiah reviews the history of Israel from the perspective of Israel's commitment to the covenant. Viewed from this perspective, it is a history of ingratitude and unfaithfulness. The indictment comes to a climax in verse 13, where Jeremiah accuses the people of forsaking him who is "the spring of living water," to hew out for themselves "broken cisterns that cannot hold water."

In other passages, Jeremiah recalls the true meaning of circumcision—the act of initiation into God's covenant people. He equates circumcision with obedience when he says of the people of the southern kingdom: "their ears are [uncircumcised] so they cannot hear" (6:10). Elsewhere he even says that God will punish both the circumcised Jews and the uncircumcised nations because they have not practiced "kindness, justice and righteousness" (9:24)—all qualities that constitute the heart of the covenant and sum up the central message of the prophets. The descendants of Abraham may go through the ritual of circumcision, but they ignore its inner meaning: the response that it calls for. Something radically new must take place. The human heart must be circumcised.

Josiah's Reform

Not long after Jeremiah begins to preach, Assyria loses control over Palestine. His hands untied, King Josiah is able to carry out his religious reform measures. They amount to a radical purification of Yahweh worship (2 Kings 23:4-14, 24). Josiah closes down local shrines of Yahweh throughout his kingdom and centralizes all public worship in Jerusalem.

Though the reform produces many good results, it fails to produce a thoroughgoing repentance. It heightens religious activities, but God is not blinded by incense smoke that he cannot see (7:9-11). The heart of God's demand is obedience, not busy religion.

On more than one occasion, Jeremiah complains that no real repentance has come of Josiah's reform, but only a more elaborate cult (6:16-21), and that the rich and powerful are using the cult as a smokescreen for their violations of a covenant law (7:1-15). He sees how impotent a reform is to change the human heart and repudiates the sufficiency of ritual sacrifice in a way the priesthood cannot approve (7:21-23).

In the year 609 B.C. tragedy strikes. Josiah dies and Judah loses its independence. Popular pagan practice return (7:16-18; 11:9-13) and public morality deteriorates. Something more radical than Josiah's reform is needed.

A New Covenant

As Israel's history moves toward the Babylonian exile, Jeremiah becomes aware that Israel is unable to repent of itself. "Can the Ethiopian change his skin or the leopard his spots? Neither can you do good who are accustomed to doing evil" (13:23). Repentance must come another way. If there is to be a national rebirth, it must have another source. Jeremiah identifies this source:

> "The time is coming," declares the LORD, "when I make a new covenant with the house of Israel and with the house of Judah. It will not be like the covenant I made with their forefathers when I took them by the hand to

lead them out of Egypt because they broke my covenant. . . . This is the covenant I will make with the house of Israel after that time," declares the LORD. "I will put my law in their minds and write it on their hearts. I will be their God, and they will be my people" (31:31-33).

God does not promise Israel a new law, but a new inward motivation and power to fulfill the law already known. The new thing is that God will inwardly motivate and empower his people. People will have the will of God in their hearts, and will desire only to do God's will.

Jeremiah is well aware that the human heart is "deceitful above all things and beyond care" (17:9), and that "it is not for man to direct his steps" (10:23). Only in the light of this devastating acknowledgment of Israel's incapacity to repent on its own strength are we able to see how radically new Yahweh's announcement is. Under the new covenant, "people will obey God not because they are supposed to but because they want to. This time no fingers will be crossed behind one's back; this time 'doing what comes naturally' will be doing what God wills. This is the miracle." (William L. Holladay, *Jeremiah: Spokesman Out of Time,* p. 119).

Jeremiah's Significance

As measured by worldly standards, Jeremiah was a failure. His message was completely ignored, and he did not succeed in preventing his people from following a suicidal course. Nevertheless, "few men cast a longer shadow over his people's history than did he; perhaps more than any other one person he enabled them to survive the disaster which had overtaken them. In a true, though limited, sense Jeremiah was a savior of Israel" (Bright, *Jeremiah,* cxii).

The fall of Jerusalem in 587 B.C. and the Babylonian exile that followed were spiritual as well as political catastrophes. According to popular belief, Jerusalem was inviolable. Though a foreign invader might lay waste Judah and even besiege Jerusalem, Jerusalem itself would not fall. Not because of the thickness of its walls, but because it was safely sheltered in the shadow of God's wings. Yahweh would not allow it to happen. He had too much invested in Jerusalem; he had made an eternal covenant with David (2 Sam. 7:4-17).

In Jeremiah's day, belief in Jerusalem's inviolability had hardened into a dogma. The notion that the city of David would fall and the Davidic dynasty cease to rule was simply not entertained. Therefore, when Jerusalem did fall and the line of Davidic kings did come to an end, popular piety and official theology were at a loss to explain it. Had Israel not been able to find an adequate explanation of the tragedy in terms of Yahweh's faithfulness to his side of the covenant agreement, it would, humanly speaking, not have survived. "That this did not occur was due in no small measure to men such as Jeremiah . . . who gave the tragedy explanation in terms of Israel's faith, and pointed the way beyond it" (Bright, *Jeremiah,* cxiii).

Five: God Pleads with His People

Chapter Review Questions

1. What is the role of a prophet?

2. But aren't future predictions part of the prophet's message?

3. How do prophets relate to God's covenant with Israel?

4. Describe the new covenant Jeremiah speaks of in Jeremiah 31:31-34.

5. Did God in fact make this new covenant? See Romans 7:6.

General Discussion Questions

1. Which passages in Jeremiah support the thesis that "the fundamental experience of the prophet is a fellowship with the feelings of God" (A. J. Heschel)?

2. Read Jeremiah 20:7-18. What type of piety does Jeremiah exhibit here? What is your reaction to it?

3. What is the central vision of the Bible as described in Micah 4:1-5?

4. What is the book of Habakkuk all about?

5. How would you conclude the Old Testament if you were asked to do so?

Notes

Six: God Promises His People a Holy City

The Birth of Judaism

The fall of Jerusalem in July 587 marked a major turning point in the history of God's people. Israel's organized national life came to an end and the history of Judaism began. Judah, the last remaining part of Israel, ceased to exist as a nation and became a religious community.

Judah's political extinction had a shattering impact on the faith of the people. Hadn't God entered into a special covenant with Israel through David the king, a covenant that guaranteed the continuity of the Davidic dynasty (2 Sam. 7)? Hadn't the story of God's mighty acts, begun in the Exodus, climaxed in God's choice of David as king and of Jerusalem as his earthly residence? Though God had rejected the northern tribes, wasn't it true that "he chose the tribe of Judah, Mount Zion, which he loved," and that "he chose David his servant" (Ps. 78:68, 70)?

If God had done all these things, why then had he allowed the temple to be destroyed and the Davidic royal house to come to an end? The deep anguish caused by this question is movingly expressed by the poet of Psalm 89:

> But you have rejected,
>   you have spurned,
>   you have been very angry with your anointed one.
> You have renounced the covenant with your servant
>   and have defiled his crown in the dust.
> You have broken through all his walls
>   and reduced his strongholds to ruins. . . .
> You have put an end to his splendor
>   and cast his throne to the ground. . . .
> Lord, where is your former great love
>   which in your faithfulness you swore to David?
>   (v. 38-49)

The danger that the southern exiles, like the northern exiles before them, would be absorbed by the Gentile population surrounding them was not at all imaginary. Judah's survival depended on its ability to change from nation into religious community. This change Judah managed to make. It "both survived the calamity and, forming a new community out of the wreckage of the old, resumed [its] life as a people. [Judah's] faith, disciplined and strengthened, likewise survived and gradually found the direction that it would follow through all the centuries to come. In the exile and beyond it, Judaism was born" (Bright, *A History of Israel*, p. 323).

The Rebuilding of the Temple

The future for which the faithful among the exiles hoped was the eventual return to the homeland. That hope was realized in 538 B.C. The year before, Babylon had fallen into the hands of the Persian king Cyrus. In 538 Cyrus allowed the Jews to return home and gave them permission to rebuild the temple in Jerusalem.

The story is told in Ezra 1:2-4 and 6:3-5. Here we read that Cyrus's decree liberally provided that the temple be rebuilt and the expenses paid from the royal treasury. Instructions were also given to restore the gold and silver vessels taken by Nebuchadnezzar and to return them to Jerusalem.

The community of repatriates was at first very small. "Though other groups of returning exiles followed the initial party in the succeeding years, by 522 the total population of Judah, including those already resident there, can scarcely have been much above 20,000. Jerusalem itself, still thinly populated seventy-five years later (Nehemiah 7:4), remained largely a ruin" (Bright, *History*, p. 347).

The repatriates faced a number of hardships. The first harvests were inadequate (Haggai 1:9-11; 2:15-17), the cost of living was high, and the wages were low. Neighbors, especially the Samaritan aristocracy, who regarded Judah as part of their territory, were openly hostile. Besides, the Judaites who had remained in Palestine were not at all enthusiastic about the return of the exiles, for these Judaites had taken over the fields and vineyards and had moved into the houses that had not been destroyed. Finally, the exiles were not coming back to their own free country, but to a province of the Persian Empire.

When the Jews left Babylon, they thought that great things would happen as soon as they reached Palestine. But it was all very disappointing. After the initial excitement of homecoming had died down, there was nothing but hardship and hostility. The dreams of restoring David's former empire and destroying all the enemies of God's people very soon faded away.

It is not surprising, therefore, that the work of rebuilding the temple, begun soon after the return, came to a halt. The people, fighting just to exist, had neither the resources nor the energy to continue the project. And the financial aid promised by the Persians evidently never amounted to much. Eighteen years after work on the temple had begun, it had not progressed beyond the foundations.

For this era, too, God had his spokesmen on the scene to proclaim the message of his coming and of his kingdom. The prophets Haggai and Zechariah appeared. Both men closely linked their message to rebuilding the temple—so closely that to them the rebuilding of the temple was actually the precondition of God's coming. The temple, after all, was the place where God spoke to Israel and where he forgave its sins; the attitude taken towards the temple betrayed the attitude for or against God. Haggai, therefore, can keep silent no longer:

> "Is it a time for you yourselves to be living in your paneled houses, while this house remains a ruin?"

> Now this is what the Lord Almighty says: "Give careful thought to your ways. You have planted much, but have harvested little. You eat, but never have enough. You drink, but never have your fill. You put on clothes, but are not warm. You earn wages, only to put them in a purse with holes in it (1:4-6).

Translated into New Testament language, Haggai's message reads: Seek first God's kingdom and his righteousness, and all the things you need to live shall be yours as well.

The result of Haggai's appeal was that "the whole remnant of the people . . . came and began to work on the house of the LORD" (1:14). In 515 the temple was finished and dedicated with much festivity (Ezra 6:13-18). God's people once more had a worship center.

The Renewal of the Covenant

The period from the completion of the temple until the middle of the next century is one of historical silence. We know almost nothing of what happened to the Jews during that time. Then, at the end of this period, Nehemiah and Ezra made their appearance. Nehemiah gave the community political status and administrative reform, and Ezra reorganized and reformed its spiritual life. The date of Nehemiah's career is certain: 445-433; the date of Ezra's career is not.

Nehemiah's Role

Nehemiah served as cupbearer at the court of the Persian king Artaxerxes. It was this king's desire to stabilize conditions in Palestine. After Nehemiah heard of the deplorable conditions there, he resolved to use his high rank to approach the king and ask for permission to go to Jerusalem with authority to rebuild its walls. His request was granted. "A rescript was granted authorizing the building of the city's walls and directing that materials for the purpose be provided from the royal forests. More than that, either at once or subsequently, Nehemiah was appointed governor of Judah (Nehemiah 5:14; 10:1), which was made a separate province independent of Samaria" (Bright, *History,* p. 364f.).

Nehemiah arrived in Jerusalem by 440 at the very latest. Immediately he took charge of affairs. As the new governor, he addressed himself first to the most urgent problem: physical security. Within fifty-two days (Neh. 6:15) a wall of some sort was up.

Nehemiah served two terms as governor of Judah. He gave the Jewish community physical security, an honest administration, and political status. What he did not do was reform its inner life. This task was reserved for Ezra, "the priest, a teacher of the Law of the God of heaven" (Ezra 7:12).

Ezra's Role

Like Nehemiah, Ezra was commissioned by Artaxerxes (Ezra 7:12-26). He was empowered to teach the law and to set up administrative machinery to see that the law was obeyed. All who claimed allegiance to the temple community of Jerusalem were ordered to conduct their affairs in accordance with the law which Ezra brought with him. This law was the Pentateuch—the first five books of the Old Testament. To disobey that law was to also disobey the law of the Persian king: "Whoever does not obey the law of your God and the law of the king must surely be punished by death, banishment, confiscation of property, or imprisonment" (Ezra 7:26).

The dramatic story of Ezra's reform is told in Nehemiah 8-10. In a great public assembly the law is read "from daybreak till noon" (8:3), and all the people, both men and women, are asked to swear allegiance to the law. Specifically, the people bind themselves to enter into no more marriages with foreigners, to refrain from work on the Sabbath, to let the land lie fallow and forego collection of debts every seventh year, and to levy on themselves an annual tax for the maintenance of the temple.

The eager expectation of God's imminent coming recedes into the background. The observance of the law begins to take the central place.

Ezra's reform program seems to have been completed within a year after his arrival in Jerusalem. Then we hear no more of him. But during his brief stay in Jerusalem he reconstituted Israel and gave its faith a form in which it could survive through the centuries. Within the framework of the political stability provided by Nehemiah, Ezra organized the Jewish community around the law, the Torah. From this time on, the distinguishing mark of a Jew would be neither national existence nor ethnic peculiarity, but adherence to the law. The law opened a way to overcome the ethnic and geographical limitations of former days. It could accompany the Jews wherever they went.

The Encouragement from History

As you may recall, the books of Samuel and Kings form a continuous story of about five hundred years of Israelite history. Beginning with the last of the judges, Samuel, they close with the last of the kings of Judah, Jehoiachin, being freed from prison by the Babylonian king and invited to dine regularly at the king's table.

When we turn to 1 Chronicles, the book immediately following 2 Kings in our English Bible, we might reasonably expect the story to continue. So far in our reading of the Old Testament, from Genesis to Kings, the narration of God's mighty acts has been continuous. However, the first book of Chronicles takes us back to the very beginning—to Adam. Then, after nine chapters of lists of names, we come to the story of Saul's death (which we already have read in 1 Samuel 31). In the remaining chapters, 1 Chronicles tells of David's accomplishments as king. The second book of Chronicles tells the story of Solomon and of all the kings of Judah, and carries the story somewhat further forward than the second book of Kings does. It ends with Cyrus, king of Persia, ordering the rebuilding of the temple in Jerusalem. Not until we begin reading the next Bible book, Ezra, do we move forward again in the history of Israel.

Why is the history of Israel repeated? Why does Chronicles traverse the story of earlier books and especially of Samuel and Kings?

Neither of these series of books was written merely to chronicle the past. Both recall the past for a special purpose. Like all good historical writing, each of these narratives was written to convey a certain message. The books of Samuel and Kings tell of the rise and fall of the Hebrew kingdom from a certain perspective. Their purpose is to answer the question: Why did Israel as a nation come to a tragic end? The reign of each king is evaluated according to whether he was faithful to Yahweh. And this account of centuries of kingdom history gradually builds into a massive confession of guilt. Israel is called to confess its sins so that God might forgive and open before it a new future.

The author of Chronicles writes from a different perspective. This author wishes to encourage the Jews who, after returning from exile, are struggling to maintain their existence against unfavorable odds.

The tone of Samuel and Kings is basically prophetic. They tell us that the history of the monarchy is intertwined with the history of prophecy. The first king is confronted by a prophet. So is David, the second king. And on several occasions we read of prophets who interfere with the course of history (1 Kings 12:21-24; 13; 14:1-8; 16:1-4). In Chronicles, on the other hand, the prophets receive very little emphasis.

In brief, the earlier history, Samuel-Kings, is written to call the nation to repentance of its past sins and to show that God always does great things for his people when they turn to him; the later history, Chronicles, is intended to reassure the people of Judah that in spite of their sinful past they are indeed the people whom God has chosen to carry out his purpose in history. Looking back over their seven-hundred-year history, how can they possibly be discouraged, seeing that God has done such great things for them?

Accordingly, Chronicles gives a history of Judah, with special reference to the institutions connected with the temple. The genealogies in 1 Chronicles 1 show the position taken by the tribe of Judah relative to other nations. The second chapter of 1 Chronicles is devoted entirely to the tribe of Judah and the third chapter to the descendants of King David.

After nine chapters of introduction, the history proper begins. The reign of Saul is quickly passed over. Thereafter 1 Chronicles narrates David's election as king over all Israel, omitting as irrelevant to its purpose the stories of his checkered activities in Judah and with the Philistines. We are told nothing about Bathsheba and nothing about his humiliation due to Absalom's rebellion. The David of Chronicles is a model king. He and his son do not rule in Israel, but in the "kingdom of the LORD" (1 Chron. 28:5). Unlike Samuel-Kings, Chronicles is not interested in showing the sins of David and Solomon. Rather, it seeks to focus attention on these men as carriers of divine promise and symbols of hope.

In Chronicles' description of David we begin to see the vague outline of the future king of Israel from David's house, who came to Jerusalem, "humble, and mounted on an ass" (Matt. 21:5). Here we detect a confluence of the pictures of David and Christ, the Son of David.

To read an account of Israel's history with this redemptive focus is a comforting experience. Chronicles gave the Jews what they needed: a renewed sense of the importance of their mission to the peoples of the world.

The Transformation of Jerusalem

The theme of Haggai's and Zechariah's prophecies is the end-time transformation of the temple and Jerusalem:

> "Shout and be glad, O daughter of Zion. For I am coming and I will live among you," declares the LORD. "Many nations will be joined with the LORD in that day and will become my people" (Zech. 2:10f.).

This particular theme has a long history. To understand its influence on Haggai's and Zechariah's message, it is necessary to trace the theme to its earliest prophetic roots.

According to the account in 1 Chronicles 11, the first thing David did after he became king of Israel was to capture the city of Jerusalem. He then had the ark—symbol of Yahweh's covenant with Israel—brought to his new capital. No decision has had greater consequences for this city; it made Jerusalem the worship center of the people of Israel. Because of the presence of the ark, Jerusalem became more than the capital and the royal residence. It was elevated to a holy city, to God's dwelling place.

In the course of time the sanctity of the ark was transferred, first to the temple and then to the city of Jerusalem as a whole. Even after the ark had been stolen and the temple destroyed, Jerusalem remained the focus of Jewish piety.

The fact that Jerusalem had been declared a holy city did not, however, change moral conditions in the city. It remained, like all other major cities, a sinful city. Jerusalem was a city built with blood (Mic. 3:10), a lodging place of murderers (Isa. 1:21), a city of great pride that insulted heaven by stubbornly following the desires of its own heart (Jer. 13:9f.). It was a city filled with injustice (Isa. 1:21).

Jerusalem was neither built by God nor for him. It was not holy in and by itself. Why not? Because holiness is not an impersonal force but a personal quality. It resides, not in the grain of matter, but in the nature of human acts. Hence, the God of the Scripture is more concerned with human conduct than with streets and buildings. God's primary concern is holy conduct, not sacred space.

If Jerusalem is to be called holy, it is only because its people reflect the holiness of God.

Deeply distressed about the unholiness of Jerusalem, the prophet Isaiah has a dream (Isa. 2:1-4). In this dream he witnesses the transformation of Jerusalem. This transformation proceeds in several stages.

First, a change takes place in the physical landscape. The temple mountain rises and is exalted above all the hills around it, so that it becomes visible to all the people in the world.

Second, the prophet sees many peoples streaming to the temple from every possible direction, peoples that no longer can cope with the desperate conditions under which they are living. Societal disorders and international violence ("swords," "spears," "wars") force these peoples to go to Jerusalem to escape from their chaotic way of life. Upon arrival in Jerusalem they receive the law: "The law will go out from Zion, the word of the LORD from Jerusalem" (Isa. 2:3).

Just as bands of Israelite pilgrims made an annual journey to Jerusalem to listen to Yahweh's will in the covenant law, so Isaiah expects that "in the last days" the nations will present themselves in Jerusalem for a final settlement of all disputes. They will subject their lives to the will of God and organize their lives in keeping with his will, beating "their swords into plowshares and their spears into pruning hooks" (2:4).

A more elaborate form of this pilgrimage prophecy is found in Isaiah 60. Like Isaiah 2, Isaiah 60 speaks of the transformation of Jerusalem. Yahweh calls on Jerusalem to awake in anticipation of the glory that he will bring. Pictured as a woman lying prostrate on the ground, Jerusalem is told to rise and reflect the light that has been shed on it from above. So bright is this light that it has the same effect as in Isaiah 2. Nations dwelling in darkness see the light of the new age from afar and come from all directions to pay tribute to the divine glory now revealed on earth. Jerusalem emerges from its previous insignificance and sets in motion a pilgrimage of the nations (60:3). Ships come sailing from the West like flights of doves. Caravans bring gold and frankincense for the temple from the East. The abundance of the sea and the wealth of the nations come to Jerusalem (60:5). Violence and social injustice cease (60:14). The sun and moon have outlived their usefulness, for Yahweh is Jerusalem's everlasting light (60:19f.). Its walls are Salvation; the gates are Praise (60:18). All the people in it are righteous (60:21). They are called "the City of the LORD, Zion of the Holy one of Israel" (60:14).

With the statement that in end-time Jerusalem all the people shall be righteous (60:21), Isaiah reached the climax of his vision. The prophet hungers and thirsts for a Jerusalem in which righteousness dwells. But only

God's indwelling presence will bring this about. Only God's presence will rid the city of its shadows and evils and make it "the everlasting pride and the joy of all generations" (60:15).

It is this Isaian pilgrimage prophecy that Haggai uses to address the Jewish community in Jerusalem. From it, however, he selects only one feature—that of the nations bringing gifts to Yahweh. Against all visible evidence he sees his time as one of salvation. Even in the poor conditions of his time he sees Yahweh as preparing for his coming to Jerusalem:

> "In a little while I will once more shake the heavens and the earth, the sea and the dry land. I will shake all nations, and the desired of all nations will come, and I will fill this house with glory," says the LORD Almighty (Hag. 2:6f.).

Haggai envisions the time when all the nations will go on a pilgrimage to Jerusalem to bring Yahweh their treasures, for he alone has a rightful claim to all the valuables which now lie scattered among the nations. "The silver is mine and the gold is mine," declares the LORD Almighty (Hag. 2:8). It is for this time, when all treasures will revert to their rightful owner, that the temple has to be rebuilt.

Zechariah, too, utilizes the Isaian pilgrimage prophecy to describe the coming of Yahweh. He speaks of the whole land being turned into a plain and of Jerusalem being exalted above it (14:10). He promises that Jerusalem will then be a great city overflowing its walls as God's people and Gentile nations (2:10f.; 8:22), or what is left of them (14:16), flock to it from all over the world. Jerusalem in that day shall be called "the City of Truth" (8:3). Everything and everyone shall be "HOLY TO THE LORD" (14:20f.). The city shall have no walls, for the glory of Yahweh "will be a wall of fire around it" (2:5).

The new Jerusalem of prophetic hope, in other words, is the end-time congregation of the faithful, a holy community that will be like a hilltop city whose light, the light of the indwelling God, will be visible to the whole world.

Six: God Promises His People a Holy City

Chapter Review Questions

1. What basic change did the fall of Jerusalem in 587 B.C. trigger in the life of God's people?

2. What, initially, kept the returned exiles from rebuilding the temple?

3. What crucial role did Nehemiah play in post-exilic Jerusalem?

4. What role did Ezra play in post-exilic Jerusalem?

5. How does the book of Chronicles tell the story of Israel differently than the books of Samuel and Kings? What might account for this difference?

6. What is wrong with calling Jerusalem a holy city? See Isaiah 2:1-4 and Isaiah 60.

General Discussion Questions

1. Chapters 8 through 10 of the book of Nehemiah describe the official birth of Judaism. How would you summarize these chapters?

2. In Malachi's day, the people were saying, "It is futile to serve God. What did we gain by carrying out his requirements and going about like mourners before the LORD Almighty? But now we call the arrogant blessed. Certainly the evildoers prosper, and even those who challenge God escape" (Mal. 3:14-15). In their poverty God's people had offered sacrifices to rebuild the temple. But who had grown rich? The evildoers! So why be concerned any longer with such an unjust God? Why continue to serve God if there is no profit in it? People became discouraged and were ready to give up their faith. Then Malachi's voice is heard. Check Malachi 1:8, 2:8, and 2:11 for his message. How is this message relevant for today?

3. How does the vision of Zechariah 4, addressed to post-exilic Judah, still speak to us today?

4. What vision of the future do you read in Zechariah 14:20-21?

Notes

Seven: The Wise Seek God

What Is Wisdom?

The book of Proverbs, Job, and Ecclesiastes belong to a special form of literature: wisdom literature. Wisdom has to do with what everyone knows and no one understands. It is interested in the routine and ordinary. It searches for laws that control familiar and everyday events. From the chaos of these events it seeks to distill some kind of order. Its purpose is to make life more predictable and therefore more secure and enjoyable.

Who were the men of wisdom? In Jeremiah 18:18 the wise are mentioned as a distinct class, along with the priests and the prophets. "They said, 'Come, let's make plans against Jeremiah; for the teaching of the law by the priest will not be lost, nor will counsel from the wise, nor the word from the prophets.'"

Originally, during the monarchy, the wise were a class of government officials, advisors, and diplomats who assisted the king, acting as a sort of advisory council. One of their responsibilities was preparing the sons of the nobility to exercise roles of political and cultural leadership. A significant part of this training consisted of memorization. It is believed that parts of the book of Proverbs are collections of sayings put together as texts to be studied, copied for practice in writing, and memorized.

The pursuit of wisdom, of course, was not unique to Israel. Contemporary Egyptian and Mesopotamian literature give evidence of a similar pursuit. Still, the Hebrew search for wisdom differed essentially from that of neighboring countries. For Israel everything was controlled by Yahweh; all spheres of life were encompassed by the power of Yahweh. For Israel, wisdom was a response to daily occurrences, conditioned by the knowledge of Yahweh's control over creation. Hence, characteristic of Israel's wise men is their "fear of Yahweh":

> The fear of the LORD is the beginning of knowledge;
> but fools despise wisdom and discipline (Prov. 1:7).
> The fear of the LORD is the beginning of wisdom,
> and knowledge of the Holy One is understanding (Prov. 9:10).
> The fear of the LORD teaches a man wisdom,
> and humility comes before honor (Prov. 15:33).

Fear, in this context, is not a feeling of fright. Rather, it means faith in the LORD, commitment to the LORD. The phrase "the fear of the LORD is the beginning of knowledge" contains in a nutshell the whole Israelite theory of knowledge. It means that there can be no true knowledge without faith in the LORD. Such faith "does not—as is popularly believed today—hinder knowledge; on the contrary, it is what liberates knowledge, enables it really to come to the point and indicates to it its proper place in the sphere of varied, human activity. In Israel, the intellect never freed itself from or became independent of the foundation of its whole existence, that is its commitment to Yahweh" (Gerhard von Rad, *Wisdom in Israel,* p. 68).

The Book of Proverbs

Since the wisdom movement originally flourished in the circles of the royal court, many of the proverbs reflect conditions at court. Because the wise originally were advisors to the king, it was necessary for them to know how to behave in the presence of royalty and nobility. Repeatedly, therefore, we come across instructions on proper conduct at the king's table, as in Proverbs 23:1f.:

> When you sit to dine with a ruler,
> note well what is before you,
> and put a knife to your throat
> if you are given to gluttony.

Wise men were often called upon to give advice to their king in a few, well-chosen words. Thus, the many instructions about the right and wrong use of words. For example,

> A man finds joy in giving an apt reply—
> and how good is a timely word! (15:23).
> A word aptly spoken
> is like apples of gold in settings of silver (25:11).

The teachings of Israel's wise men are all composed in poetic form. In fact, they are poetry. This combination of wisdom and poetry is not incidental but essential, for by their choice and arrangement of words poets bring thoughts to sharpest focus. Let's look at some of the literary forms which these men used to express their wisdom.

Parallelisms

The most basic literary form in Israel is parallelism. It consists of two parallel lines. In these, the poet is forced to express his thought from two points of view. Parallelisms come in various kinds. The three most frequently occurring kinds are the synonymous parallelism, the antithetic parallelism, and the synthetic parallelism.

In the synonymous parallelism the two lines say approximately the same thing. Examples are

How much better to get wisdom than gold,
    to choose understanding rather than silver! (16:16).
A fool's mouth is his undoing,
    and his lips are a snare to his soul (18:7).

In the antithetic parallelism the two lines say the opposite thing. Examples are

Misfortune pursues the sinner,
    but prosperity is the reward of the righteous (13:21).
A wise son brings joy to his father,
    but a foolish son grief to his mother (10:1).

Since the contrast provided by the second line is not the precise opposite, antithetic parallelisms provide endless possibilities of variation. The poet furnishes only one possible opposite among many. To familiarize yourself with Hebrew poetry, you might try to supply different opposites from the ones you find in, for example, Proverbs 10-16.

In the synthetic parallelism the second line says neither the same as the first line nor the opposite, but adds to the thought of the first line. This kind of parallelism, too, provides endless variations. Examples are

The name of the LORD is a strong tower;
    the righteous run to it and are safe (18:10).
The tongue has the power of life and death,
    and those who love it will eat its fruit (18:21).

Numerical Proverbs

Another literary form in which Israel expressed its wisdom is the so-called numerical proverb. This kind of proverb gives expression to the basic human urge to list things or people that belong to the same category. Example:

There are six things the Lord hates,
    seven that are detestable to him:
haughty eyes,
    a lying tongue,
    hands that shed innocent blood,
a heart that devises wicked schemes,
    feet that are quick to run into evil,
a false witness who pours out lies
    and a man who stirs up dissension among brothers (6:16-19).

Numerical sayings list things or people whose similarity is not immediately obvious and comes as a surprise. As such, they come close to being riddles and easily lend themselves to being changed into riddles. And riddles, as we learn from Proverbs 1:6, were used by wisdom teachers. They would hide the truth in a riddle and then ask their students to bring it out of hiding into the light. For example, they might ask, Which four things on earth are small, yet exceedingly wise? The answer:

Ants are creatures of little strength,
yet they store up their food in the summer;
coneys are creatures of little power,
yet they make their home in the crags;
locusts have no king,
yet they advance together in ranks;
a lizard can be caught with the hand,
yet it is found in kings' palaces (30:25-28).

The initial purpose of the wisdom movement in Israel was practical: to educate the sons of nobles for positions of leadership. This purpose, however, "is increasingly matched by a concern to say in human terms what the ultimate meaning of man's life is: what its real goal is, how this is to be attained, and by what means. In modern terms, from being a movement concerned with practical ethics it becomes a movement increasingly concerned with religious and theological issues" (J. Coert Rylaarsdam, *The Proverbs, Ecclesiastes, the Song of Solomon*, p. 10). Job and Ecclesiastes are examples of this later stage of the wisdom movement.

The Book of Job

The book of Job reflects a debate among teachers of wisdom. Job says as much in his sarcastic answer to Zophar:

Doubtless you are the people,
and wisdom will die with you!
But I have a mind as well as you;
I am not inferior to you (12:2f.).

What issue are Job and his wise friends debating? The issue of whether good behavior results in prosperity and bad behavior in suffering. Job questions this traditional formula by maintaining that he is a good man whose lot has turned from prosperity to suffering. The friends can account for Job's troubles only by denying that he is good: badness leads to suffering, and since Job is suffering, Job must be bad.

Why should a good person suffer if God is all-powerful and just? To explain this anomaly, Job's friends put forward various theories (see R. B. Y. Scott, *The Way of Wisdom*, p. 145ff.):

Suffering is *deserved punishment*. The friends assert that Job's suffering proves his sinfulness and that by pretending to be blameless he is hypocritical besides:

Consider now: Who, being innocent, has ever perished?
Where were the upright ever destroyed?
As I have seen, those who plow iniquity
and sow trouble reap the same.
By the breath of God they perish,
and by the blast of his anger they are consumed (4:7-9).

Suffering is *inevitable.* Since all people are sinners, suffering is inevitable. So says Eliphaz:

What is man, that he could be pure,
  or one born of woman, that he could be righteous?
If God places no trust in his holy ones,
  if even the heavens are not pure in his eyes,
how much less man, who is vile and corrupt,
  who drinks up evil like water! (15:14-16).

Suffering is *disciplinary.* Both Elihu and Eliphaz remind Job of the traditional interpretation of suffering: it is intended to discipline.

Blessed is the man whom God corrects;
  so do not despise the discipline of the Almighty (5:17).
But those who suffer he delivers in their suffering;
  he speaks to them in their affliction (36:15).

Suffering is *temporary.* In an effort to break Job's defiance, all three of Job's friends claim that suffering is of a temporary nature and therefore must be endured.

For he wounds, but he also binds up;
  he injures, but his hands also heal (5:18).
God does not reject a blameless man
  or strengthen the hands of evildoers.
He will yet fill your mouth with laughter
  and your lips with shouts of joy (8:20f.).
The mirth of the wicked is brief,
  the joy of the godless lasts but a moment (20:5).

Job, however, persists in his claim that he is innocent. But if he is innocent, why does God allow him to suffer?

Though I cry "I've been wronged!" I get no response;
  though I call for help, there is no justice.
He has blocked my way so I cannot pass;
  he has shrouded my paths in darkness (19:7f.).

During the period when God refrains from answering Job's questions, Job clings to three certainties that save him from total despair. First, he remembers the days when God was yet with him, when his children were about him (29:5). Second, he clings to his own integrity. God may kill me, he says, yet "I will surely defend my ways to his face" (13:15). Third, he is convinced that, if only he knew where to find God so that he could lay his case before him and argue it, God would not contend with him. "There an upright man could present his case before him, and I would be delivered forever from my judge" (23:7). Job is sure that he has a vindicator in heaven who will give him a hearing (16:19). Since God must be just or he cannot be God, Job never doubts that justice will be done to him in the end. He knows that the vindicator of his integrity lives (19:25).

In the ongoing debate, Job increasingly talks in legal terms. He pictures the universe as a court of justice where his case can be tried. He challenges God to state his accusations openly and meet him face-to-face in court:

Oh, that I had someone to hear me!
I sign now my defense—let the Almighty answer me;
let my accuser put his indictment in writing.
Surely I would wear it on my shoulder,
I would put it on like a crown;
I would give him an account of my every step;
like a prince I would approach him (31:35-37).

God answers Job from the whirlwind (38-39; 40:6-14). In a series of questions he confronts Job with the mystery of creation. These questions tell Job that it is presumptuous for a creature to pass judgment on the Creator. How can Job, as a creature, know the mind of his Maker?

Having overwhelmed Job by his wisdom and power displayed in creation, God then asks: "Will the one who contends with the Almighty correct him? Let him who accuses God answer him" (40:2). Job answers: "How can I reply to you? I put my hand over my mouth" (40:4).

None of Job's questions have been answered. Nothing has been said about suffering and justice. In the new perspective God has opened, the question, Why do I suffer? has lost its urgency. How foolish of Job to deduce from his limited experience that the whole universe is unjustly governed! "Only God can understand the dimensions of justice, for he must administer it. Has Job, or any man, the wisdom to know what justice must encompass in universal terms? Has Job really been concerned with justice, or only with justifying himself? . . . Will he now, in fact, accept the conditions of his creaturehood or does he presume he has the wisdom to mount God's throne and judge all men with a more authentic justice?" (Scott, *Wisdom,* p. 161).

The book of Job concludes with a prayer of confession in which Job accepts the mystery of God's justice:

I know that you can do all things;
no plan of yours can be thwarted. . . .
Surely I spoke of things I did not understand,
things too wonderful for me to know. . . .
My ears had heard of you
but now my eyes have seen you.
Therefore I despise myself
and repent in dust and ashes (42:2-6).

The Book of Ecclesiastes

Like Proverbs and Job, Ecclesiastes too is a product of Israel's wisdom tradition. In an effort to find a basis for purposeful living, its author searches out "by wisdom" all that is happening in the world (1:13). Guided by the discipline of wisdom, he conducts a number of experiments in living to try to uncover the meaning of life, what is "worthwhile for men to do under heaven during the few days of their lives" (2:3).

The author calls himself "the Teacher" (1:1). In our day "we would probably have called him a critic or an essayist. The main role for such a man is to analyze an established view of life, probe its standard assertions, and expose the weaknesses and superficialities covered over by a repetition of habit" (Rylaarsdam, *The Proverbs*, p. 94). Though he uses the same method which other men of wisdom use to examine the facts of life, he uses it more thoroughly and then bravely accepts the stark conclusions to which they lead.

All Is Vanity

Does wisdom, experientially discovered, offer a key to the meaning of a person's life? The Teacher answers: it does not! In the last analysis, all such wisdom is vanity—it does not penetrate the deep mystery that conceals the ways of God. And since God is the absolute sovereign over all things, human wisdom cannot clarify the meaning of life.

What the Teacher questions is not God but the human attempt to discover the purpose of all things through the discipline of wisdom. On this attempt he gives his final verdict: "Meaningless! Meaningless!" (1:2).

The Teacher's favorite way of arguing this meaninglessness is by pointing to the inescapable fact of death. Death, more than anything else, illustrates the relative nature of all that people do and have. Death casts its dark shadow over everything. It is the great leveler. It mocks all human pretensions:

> All share a common destiny—the righteous and the wicked, the good and the bad, the clean and the unclean, those who offer sacrifices and those who do not. As it is with the good man, so it is with the sinner; as it is with those who take oaths, so with those who are afraid to take them. This is the evil in everything that happens under the sun: The same destiny overtakes all (9:2-3).

Seeing that death wipes out all human distinctions, what are we to do? Is there any real value left in life? The Teacher offers this advice: Become involved. Throw yourself into life. Find satisfaction in food, clothes, marriage, and work (9:7-10). Since the discipline of wisdom does not yield a basis for meaningful living, the best we can do is enjoy such moments of happiness as God permits us to have. Our youth especially is to be treasured, for life passes quickly (12:1).

A Time for Everything

Depressing though he may sound, the Teacher is far from believing that events in the world are chaotic. He is convinced that God mysteriously governs all. To give expression to this conviction, he uses the term "time." For everything there is a proper time—

> a time to be born and a time to die,
> a time to plant and a time to uproot,
> a time to kill and a time to heal,

a time to break down and a time to build,
a time to weep and a time to laugh,
a time to mourn and a time to dance (3:2-4).

The opening statement, "a time to be born and a time to die," provides the clue to what the Teacher means. The time of birth and the time of death are not under human control. Neither are any of the other events and actions he lists. They all take place as and when it pleases God, and no human being is in a position to argue with God. "Whatever exists has already been named, and what man is has been known; no man can contend with one who is stronger than he" (6:10).

God is in charge of the "times." Though man proposes, God disposes. That's why "the race is not to the swift or the battle to the strong" (9:11). Just as we have nothing to say about the day of our birth and the day of our death, so behind all events in our life lies the unchangeable plan of God. Still, we should not let this fact demoralize us. Rather, we should enjoy the things that God, in the allotted times, gives us. Therefore, "when times are good, be happy; but when times are bad, consider: God has made the one as well as the other. Therefore, a man cannot discover anything about his future" (7:14).

God has a time for everything. He has an all-inclusive plan. If only we could know this plan! But we can't. It is too deeply hidden. "Whatever wisdom may be, it is far off and most profound—who can discover it?" (7:24). The hiddenness of God's plan keeps the Teacher from discovering the meaning of his life. As a result, he feels himself perpetually suspended over the abyss of meaninglessness.

At the end of this book, the Teacher repeats his basic theme: "Meaningless! . . . Everything is meaningless" (12:8). "Meaningless" is the English translation of a Hebrew word that means breath. It's like your breath on a cold morning. Now you see it, now you don't. It is without substance or permanence. The Teacher's theme may therefore be paraphrased as follows: "Everything is empty and utterly futile, like the thinnest of vapors. Fleeting as breath, it amounts to nothing. All a man's experience, his desires and his hopes, his efforts and and his accomplishments, even his righteousness and his wisdom, are transient and without result. They change nothing and they add nothing" (Scott, *Wisdom,* p. 178).

Ecclesiastes is one of the latest, if not the latest, Old Testament book to have been written. Therefore, at the close of the Old Testament period the Teacher leaves us standing in front of the wailing wall, bemoaning the futility of everything that is done under the sun.

Then, in sharp contrast, on the very first page of the New Testament, God's light shines in the darkness of this futility: an angel of the Lord announces the birth of Jesus. "You are to give him the name Jesus," the angels tell Joseph, for he will save his people from the closed cycle of destructive and meaningless living.

Seven: The Wise Seek God

Chapter Review Questions

1. What does the book of Proverbs mean by "the fear of the Lord"?

2. Why does Proverbs 1:7 mention folly and not ignorance as the opposite of wisdom?

3. Rephrase Proverbs 13:13 in your own words. What insight does it express?

4. What are some of the conventional answers to the question of why a good man like Job *should* suffer?

5. How, in Job 38-41, does God answer Job?

6. What are some of the basic insights around which Ecclesiastes clusters its ideas?

7. Since we cannot know God in the world, what, according to Ecclesiastes, are we to do?

General Discussion Questions

1. "The book of Proverbs makes Protestants feel uncomfortable." Do you agree with this statement? Why or why not?

2. Why is the author of Ecclesiastes called God's great debunker?

3. In what way does Job resemble the ostrich described in Job 39:13-18?

4. Who are the Jobs of our time?

5. Of what value to you personally are the wisdom books of Job, Proverbs, and Ecclesiastes? Of what value are such books to the life of the church today?

Notes

Eight: God Sends the Son to His People

T he Old Testament and the New make up a single volume: the Bible. The New Testament does not replace or supersede the Old. Rather, it fulfills the Old. Its opening words are: "A record of the genealogy of Jesus Christ the son of David, the son of Abraham" (Matt. 1:1). In Jesus, God fulfills what he promised to Abraham and David. Jesus is the legitimate heir of the royal throne of David and of the promises made to Abraham. In him, all of God's goals for Israel and humankind find their fulfillment.

The New Testament presents four portraits of this Jesus. In this chapter we will look at three of them.

Mark's Portrait of Jesus

Who Then Is This?

Mark writes his Gospel in such a way that it accentuates the hidden glory of God. He sets before his readers the Jesus whose divine glory is hidden from people. All the actors in Mark's Gospel, therefore, are puzzled about Jesus' identity. "Who is this?" the disciples ask after Jesus calms the waves (4:41). This question, though expressed in various ways, is on everybody's lips. The people, his enemies, his disciples, the Gentiles, the Nazareth townspeople—all sense that Jesus is more than a mere human being.

The people. In Mark 1:21, Jesus enters the Capernaum synagogue. His teaching brings him to a violent debate with an unclean spirit, and this debate leads him to expel the spirit: "Be quiet! . . . Come out of him!" (1:25). Though the unclean spirit is able to identify Jesus ("the Holy One of God"), the human spectators are not. They are merely amazed. Their blindness to Jesus' identity is revealed by their question, "What is this?"

Jesus' enemies. In Mark 3:22, teachers of the law from Jerusalem accuse Jesus of being possessed by Beelzebub. Reports have reached them that Jesus has released people from demonic possession (1:23-26, 32-34; 3:11f.). Their explanation is: Jesus casts out demons by the prince of demons, Beelzebub.

Jesus' disciples. In Mark 6:45-52, the disciples are crossing the Sea of Galilee. In the fourth watch of the night, sometime between 3:00 and 6:00 A.M., Jesus

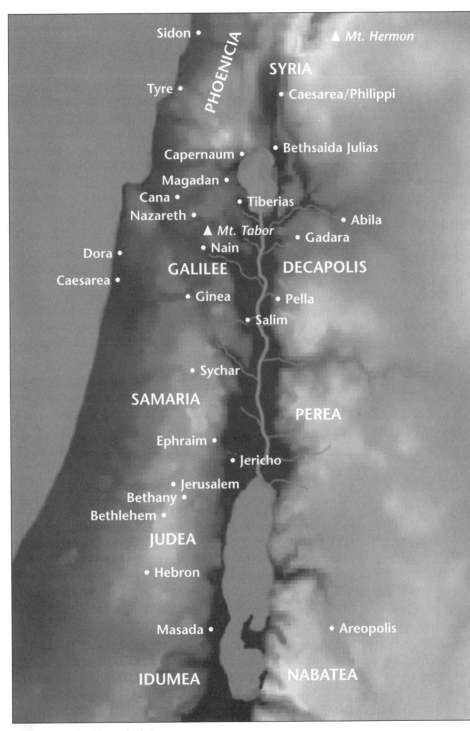

Palestine at the Time of Christ

comes to them walking on the sea. As he approaches, the disciples mistake him for a ghost or water-spirit (the Jews regarded the sea as a dwelling place of demons). Jesus allays their fears. As he gets into the boat with them, the wind ceases. The concluding statement of the story comes as a surprise: "for they had not understood about the *loaves*; their hearts were hardened" (v. 52). In this remark, Mark links the story of Jesus walking on the sea to the preceding story of the miraculous feeding (vv. 30-44). Since the disciples failed to identify Jesus after seeing him multiply the loaves, they are not now in a position to recognize him as he demonstrates his divine power by walking on the waves.

Gentiles. In Mark 5:1-20, Jesus heals a demoniac in the country of the Gerasenes. When the people from the city and country see "the man who had been possessed by the legion of demons . . . in his right mind" (v. 15), they are afraid. Afraid of what? Of Jesus' supreme power. They fear being with someone who openly combats demonic forces and therefore beg Jesus to depart from their region (v. 17). Fear closes the eyes of these Gentiles from the area of Decapolis to Jesus' identity.

Nazareth townspeople. In Mark 6:1-6, Jesus returns to his hometown. On the Sabbath he attends synagogue and teaches. Many of the congregation are astonished at his teaching and raise questions about the source of his wisdom and power. They seek to establish Jesus' identity by asking three questions. Their first question is: "Isn't this the carpenter?" A manual laborer like the rest of us? What then gives him the right to set himself up as an authority on religion? Their second question is: "Isn't this Mary's son?" In the East, a male was customarily described as a son of his father. To call one a son of his mother was derogatory. Calling Jesus the son of Mary is casting suspicions on the legitimacy of his birth. It is like saying to Jesus: "The only mystery about you is the mystery of your dubious birth." Third, the townspeople ask: "Isn't this the brother of James, Joseph, Judas, and Simon? Aren't his sisters here with us?" Jesus, they are saying, is not superhuman. He has brothers and sisters. And since they are ordinary people, how can Jesus be extraordinary? "And they took offense at him."

Who Do You Say That I Am?

The incident at Caesarea Philippi (8:27-38) marks the watershed of Mark's gospel. At last the moment arrives when Jesus lifts the veil that covers his identity. He asks, "Who do people say I am?" (v. 27). He receives various answers: John the Baptist, Elijah, one of the prophets. Though each of these answers rates Jesus very highly, the role they assign to him is one of preparation rather than of consummation. None of these answers identifies Jesus as God's final word. Jesus then asks his disciples, "Who do you say I am?" (v. 29). Peter, speaking for all of them, says, "You are the Christ." His answer rings with finality. We therefore might expect Jesus to commend Peter. Instead, Jesus charges or rebukes (the Greek word can mean both) the disciples to tell no one about him.

Why? Because of the inadequacy of the title "Messiah" as it functioned in the hope of the Jewish people at that time. This title stood for the highest political office in Judaism. The Messiah, a descendant of David, would rule the way King David ruled. He would defeat the Romans, liquidate all Gentile opposition, and lead Israel to a position of world leadership. Understandably, Jesus hurries to create distance between himself and this Führer-role. He charges the disciples not to apply it to him and then refers to himself as the Son of Man.

The use of the title "Son of Man" was an antidote to the disciples' triumphalistic Messiah. This title refers to the vision in Daniel 7. In that vision "one like a son of man" (v. 13) represents a remnant of faithful Jews who, through suffering and hardship (vv. 21, 25f.), are vindicated by God and receive a world empire (vv. 22, 27). By claiming the title "Son of Man," Jesus indicates that he thinks of himself as destined to suffer, yet one day to be brought by God out of defeat to triumph, out of death to life. As he prophesies in Mark 8:31: "the Son of Man must suffer many things and be rejected by the elders, chief priests and teachers of the law, and be killed, and after three days rise again."

Peter, his head swimming with political dreams, is shocked by the announcement that the Messiah must suffer and die. He begins to rebuke Jesus. Jesus retorts with an in-depth analysis of Peter's rebuke: it is a Satanic effort to sidetrack him from his mission. Like his fellow Jews, Peter expects a conquering Messiah. To him a suffering Messiah is a contradiction in terms. Yet it is this contradiction that Jesus presents as the heart of his mission.

This Man Was the Son of God!

Immediately after Jesus' death, the curtain of the temple is torn in two (Mark 15:38). The temple has now been rendered obsolete. The high priest is no longer necessary to gain access to God. Jesus' body broken on the cross provides such access. Now it is possible "to enter the Most Holy Place by the blood of Jesus, by a new and living way opened for us through the curtain" (Heb. 10:19f.).

The first person to benefit from this direct access is the Roman centurion in charge of the crucifixion. As the firstfruits of the great Gentile ingathering, he enters the holy place by confessing, "Surely this man was the Son of God!" (15:39). This Gentile is the first to pierce the veil that throughout the gospel of Mark has hidden Jesus' identity. He is the first to confess openly that the crucified Jesus is the Son of God.

This confession, in one respect, forms the climax of Mark's gospel. In chapter 1:1, Mark began to relate "the gospel about Jesus Christ, the Son of God." Now, in chapter 15:39, he concludes it on the same note. The truth of Jesus' divine sonship, which met with little or no positive response in Mark's gospel, now is publicly confessed by this Roman army officer. Even before Jesus' body is buried, the cross has already proven its power. It has already demonstrated that "it is the power of God for the salvation of everyone who believes" (Rom. 1:16).

They Said Nothing to Anyone

After the confession of the Roman centurion we would expect Mark to continue to write about the newly discovered identity of Jesus. The breakthrough achieved by the centurion, however, is an exception. In his final chapter, Mark does not report a believing response to Jesus' resurrection by anyone. And because we are so used to reading Mark's account of the resurrection in the light of Matthew and Luke, where there is such a believing response, we fail to hear Mark's unique message.

On Sunday morning, Mary Magdalene, Mary the mother of James, and Salome go to the tomb. Entering it, they see a young man dressed in a white robe who says to them, "You are looking for Jesus the Nazarene, who was crucified. He has risen! He is not here. See the place where they laid him. But go, tell his disciples and Peter, 'He is going ahead of you into Galilee. There you will see him, just as he told you.' "

Instead of carrying out his assignment, the three women "said nothing to anyone, because they were afraid" (16:8).

Mark concludes his gospel at this point. The verses 9-20, familiar to many of us as the conclusion of Mark in the King James Version, are now generally recognized not to be Mark's work but a compilation from a later date, written to make the story more "complete." Writes Norman Perrin: "It is the virtually unanimous opinion of modern scholarship that what appears in most translations of the gospels as Mark 16:9-20 is a pastiche of material taken from the other gospels and added to the original text of the gospel as it was copied and transmitted by the scribes of the ancient Christian communities" (*The Resurrection According to Matthew, Mark, and Luke,* p. 16).

Why does Mark end his gospel in such a strange way? Why doesn't he have the women carry out their assignment, as they do in Matthew's and Luke's gospel?

The answer is given by the entire gospel of Mark. Mark introduces the women after all the disciples have forsaken Jesus. Forsaken by them, Jesus dies. It is at this point, right after Jesus has died, that Mark introduces the women: "Some women were watching from a distance" (15:40). These women, who have not appeared in Mark's gospel before, assume the role we might have expected the disciples to play. They look on as Jesus dies. They watch where he is buried. They go to the tomb to anoint Jesus. They are the first to hear that Jesus is risen. But, like the disciples, they too fail in their mission. They say nothing to anyone. Discipleship failure, so Mark is saying, is total. As the disciples failed Jesus, so also do the women.

By ending his gospel at verse 8, Mark is saying what he has been saying all along—that all Israel failed to perceive Jesus as the Son of God and that the revelation of who Jesus is awaits the return of the risen Jesus to his own (16:7).

Matthew's Portrait of Jesus

The Synoptic Problem

The gospels of Matthew, Mark, and Luke are called the Synoptic Gospels. They are called synoptic because, when you study then synoptically, that is, in parallel columns, you can see their striking similarities, not only in wording, but also in the order of incidents. How are we to explain these similarities? This is the synoptic problem. The synoptic problem asks the question: How did the first three gospels come to be so closely related? It also asks the question: Having so much in common, why do Matthew, Mark, and Luke have so many differences?

Insofar as all three gospels present the life and teaching of Jesus, many similarities between them are to be expected. Nevertheless, the high degree of similarity in content, order, and wording demands an explanation.

The agreements in the content of the narratives. Mark, the shortest of the three, consists of 103 narratives. Of these, 98 are included in Matthew and at least 50 are included in Luke. Of the total of 661 verses in Mark, the substance of 606 verses is paralleled in Matthew and the substance of 350 verses is paralleled in Luke.

The agreements in the order of the narratives. The Synoptic Gospels largely follow the same plan. Incidents that occur in all three usually occur in approximately the same order. Where Matthew departs from Mark's order, Luke agrees with Mark. And where Luke departs from Mark's order, Matthew agrees with Mark. There is no instance where Matthew and Luke agree together against Mark's order.

The agreements in wording. Three witnesses, even when faithfully reporting the same incident, invariably tell their respective stories in a different way, using different words and expressions. Generally speaking, this phenomenon is absent from the Synoptic Gospels. Matthew uses 51 percent of Mark's actual words; Luke uses 53 percent.

The solution to the synoptic problem generally accepted by New Testament scholars is that Mark was written first and that Matthew and Luke used Mark as one of their sources. What is common to all three is due to the dependence of Matthew and Luke upon Mark. This solution is called the theory of Mark's priority. Leading Reformed New Testament scholars, such as Ned B. Stonehouse and Herman Ridderbos, accept this theory.

The King of the Kingdom

Matthew follows Mark's narrative outline very closely. This outline is geographical:

Mark 1-9—Jesus' ministry in and near Galilee
Mark 10—Jesus' journey to Jerusalem
Mark 11-13—Jesus in Jerusalem
Mark 14-16—Jesus' passion and resurrection

Like Mark, Matthew portrays Jesus as the promised Messiah, though he emphasizes the hiddenness of Jesus' Messiahship less than Mark does. But unlike Mark, who almost exclusively reports Jesus' actions, Matthew includes many of Jesus' teachings. It is especially from what he adds—a prologue, five of Jesus' discourses, and an epilogue—that we learn Matthew's particular understanding of Jesus.

A prologue (Matt. 1-2). In his opening chapter, Matthew traces Jesus' descent from Abraham through David and the members of David's dynasty who occupied the throne after David. Matthew's aim is to establish Jesus' title to the throne of David and to show that, in Jesus, God's promise to King David has reached ultimate fulfillment: "Your house and your kingdom will endure forever before me; your throne will be established forever" (2 Sam. 7:16). Therefore, when Matthew goes on to tell how the wise men from the East come to seek the newborn king of the Jews, his readers are already aware of Jesus' identity as king. Nor are they surprised that the news of Jesus' birth causes such a commotion in Jerusalem, where another king of the Jews has already been reigning for a number of years.

Five discourses. The core theme of Jesus' teaching in Matthew is the kingdom of God. In the five discourses that Matthew adds to the Marcan outline, Jesus talks about the following aspects of the kingdom:

1. *The law of the kingdom* (Matt. 5-7). In what is generally known as the Sermon on the Mount, Jesus sets forth the law of the kingdom of God. This law is not the kind that is enforceable by external sanctions. The Sermon on the Mount does not simply contain the moral commandments of Jesus. To think this is to miss the sermon's point. "We can only interpret the Sermon on the Mount in the light of Him *who lived it*. He alone can work in us the change of heart implied in every one of his commandments" (de Dietrich, *The Witnessing Community,* p. 134). It is only in the power of Christ that we can obey the Sermon on the Mount. To obey it, we must possess the qualities mentioned in the opening beatitudes (Matt. 5:3-11). We must be poor in spirit, meek, merciful, pure in heart, etc. But these are not qualities that can be enforced by law. They are identical with what Paul, in Galatians 5, calls the fruits of the Spirit. They constitute the behavior of those who belong to Christ Jesus, who "have crucified the sinful nature with its passions and desires" (Gal. 5:24).

2. *The progress of the kingdom* (Matt. 10:5-42). In this discourse, Jesus commissions the twelve apostles to proclaim by word and action the approach of the kingdom. Jesus' commission, warnings, and consolations do not apply just to the apostles, but are valid for all who in the future are called to take part in the service of the kingdom.

3. *The secret of the kingdom* (Matt. 13:1-52). In the seven parables found in Matthew 13, Jesus teaches that the kingdom of God progresses in secret. In the first parable—that of the sower—he teaches that the kingdom of God "is coming like a seed, seemingly the weakest and most defenseless thing there is. It can be devoured by the fowls; it can be choked by the thorns. It

can be scorched by the sun, and sometimes it can hardly be distinguished from the tares. That is the secret of the Kingdom. And back of this lies an even greater mystery, namely, that He who brings the Kingdom is a Sower, seemingly the most dependent of men" (Herman N. Ridderbos, *When the Time Had Fully Come*, p. 16).

4. *The fellowship of the kingdom* (Matt. 18:1-35). In this discourse Jesus sets forth the rules of conduct that should govern the life of every Christian community. Like their king, Christians should be willing to be the least and to forgive.

5. *The consummation of the kingdom* (Matt. 24:1-25:46). In this final discourse Jesus teaches that in the future everything that now resists the kingdom of God will be judged and destroyed.

An epilogue. In Matthew's account of Jesus' resurrection, Jesus is portrayed as a king with unlimited power. In Galilee, where he appears to his disciples, Jesus "speaks of his own unlimited authority (all power); he commits to them an unlimited task (all nations); he assure them of an unlimited companionship (all the days)" (Herman N. Ridderbos, *Matthew's Witness to Jesus Christ*, p. 94). Jesus, the king of the kingdom of God, calls the church to stand in the power, in the task, and in the promise of the kingdom. He calls it to do so "to the very end of the age."

John's Portrait of Jesus

John's purpose in writing his gospel is "that you may believe that Jesus is the Christ, the Son of God, and that by believing you may have life in his name" (John 20:31). John makes two statements regarding Jesus: he is the Christ, the Son of God; he brings life.

Jesus Is the Christ, the Son of God

John wrote his gospel towards the end of the first century. At that time the center of Christianity had shifted from Palestine to the Greek-Roman world. Jewish Christianity had become somewhat of a backwater, and Gentile Christianity was becoming the mainstream. The more Christianity grew on Gentile soil, the less important became the place where the gospel stories had originated. The earthly, historical Jesus became less important; the heavenly eternal Christ more important.

John wrote his gospel to unite the Jesus of Nazareth and the living Christ. He never allows us to rest in history. But neither does he allow us to rest in what is beyond history. Throughout his gospel we find ourselves in a field of tension between the historical Jesus and the heavenly Christ. The heavenly Christ is known only to those who believe in the historical Jesus. And Jesus of Nazareth is known only to those who confess him to be the Word that in the beginning was with God.

This perspective explains why John refers to Jesus' mighty acts as "signs," not as miracles or wonders. A sign, by its very nature, points away from itself. Its true meaning lies beyond itself. The signs Jesus performs in John 2-12 are pointers to who Jesus is. For example, Jesus' miracle at the wedding in Cana (2:1-11) is a sign, in that water changed into wine points to Jesus. "Water serves until this time for the purification rites of the Jews. In place of all these rites there comes now the wine of the Lord's Supper, the blood of Christ. The purification from sin is no longer achieved by following these laws, but in the Lord's Supper in which Christ the 'Lamb of God' offers forgiveness of sins to believers, through his death on the Cross" (Oscar Cullmann, *Early Christian Worship*, p. 70).

Another example. After Jesus provides bread for the hungry crowds, he explains the meaning of what he has done in these words: "I am the living bread that came down from heaven. If anyone eats of this bread, he will live forever" (6:51). The physical bread that fed the five thousand is a sign. It points to Jesus, who came down from heaven that people might never hunger again.

Jesus Brings Life

There is one basic theme binding all the stories in John's gospel together: Jesus brings life to those who are in the power of death. The healing of the sick, the feeding of the hungry, the giving of sight to the blind, the raising of Lazarus—all are manifestations of the life-giving ministry of Jesus. He came "that they may have life, and have it to the full" (10:10). Jesus himself is the life (11:25). To believe in Jesus is to have (eternal) life (5:24).

Jesus' life-giving ministry reaches its climax in his suffering and death. Jesus brings life through his death. From his death, life is released, truly and fully. Where from a human point of view life grinds to a halt, there from God's point of view life flows most abundantly. Hence, John's gospel moves toward, and culminates in, Jesus' passion and resurrection. Not until Jesus dies is life fully manifested. Jesus' crucifixion, therefore, "is not a defeat needing the Resurrection to serve it, but a victory which the Resurrection quickly follows and seals" (Michael Ramsey, *The Resurrection of Christ,* p. 20).

Following his resurrection, Jesus calls upon his disciples to continue his life-giving ministry to the world. "He breathed on them, and said, 'Receive the Holy Spirit' " (20:22). The words "he breathed on them" recall Genesis 2:7, where, after having formed man of dust from the ground, God breathes into his nostrils the breath of life and the man becomes a living being.

In John 20:22, the risen Jesus breathes into his disciples the breath of life, and they become a living and life-giving fellowship.

Eight: God Sends the Son to His People

Chapter Review Questions

1. The question of who Jesus really is is the glue that holds the gospel of Mark together. What three answers to that question can be found in Mark 1:1?

2. How does the gospel of Mark treat the issue of Jesus' identity as king? Compare this treatment with how Jesus' kingship is handled in Matthew and Luke.

3. How does Mark's story of Jesus' resurrection differ from those of Paul and the other gospel writers?

4. What does Jesus mean by the kingdom of God or the kingdom of heaven?

5. What is John's purpose in writing his gospel?

6. How does the story of Jesus' crucifixion in John differ from that in other gospels?

General Discussion Chapters

1. If Mark was the first gospel to be written, why is it not the first gospel in the New Testament?

2. Do the gospels present us with a biography of Jesus? Explain.

3. Why does Jesus use parables to teach about God and his kingdom (see Mark 4:34)?

4. Why does John call the acts of Jesus "signs"?

5. The story in John 20:19-29 sounds very liturgical. Do you recognize elements that continue in our liturgical traditions today?

6. We have been looking at what the gospels tell us about Jesus. That does not, of course, answer the question of who Jesus is to you. Imagine Jesus asking you personally, "Who do you say that I am?" Take a moment to reflect on this. Then, if you wish, share your response with the group.

Notes

Nine: God Gathers All His People

The gospel of Luke and the Acts of the Apostles are two volumes of a single work. Acts is a continuation of the gospel of Luke. It opens with the words, "In my former book, Theophilus, I wrote about all that Jesus began to do and to teach" (1:1). This "former book" that Luke refers to is his gospel. These two volumes were first separated by the gospel of John when the New Testament canon was formed in the second century.

A single theme runs through this single work of Luke-Acts: Jesus brings the salvation of God to the whole world; he creates a worldwide fellowship in which the distinction between Jew and Gentile is obsolete. Where does this salvation begin? At the beginning of Luke's gospel, in the temple of Jerusalem, where an angel appears to Zechariah and promises that the forerunner of the Messiah will be born. Where does it end? At the end of Acts, in Rome, where for two years Paul preaches the kingdom of God and teaches about the Lord Jesus Christ. Luke's one story begins at the center of Jewry—the temple—and ends in the capital of the empire—Rome.

The Gospel According to Luke

The Purpose of Jesus' Ministry

Jesus announces the purpose of his ministry in his inaugural sermon in the synagogue at Nazareth. Here he publishes his commission to bring in God's year of Jubilee, the year that was to see the end of all oppression and bondage. Jesus states that he has come to fulfill Isaiah 61:1:

> The Spirit of the sovereign LORD is on me, because the LORD has anointed me to preach good news to the poor. He has sent me to bind up the brokenhearted, to proclaim freedom for the captives and release from darkness for the prisoners, to proclaim the year of the LORD's favor.

At first the people respond with enthusiasm. They speak well of Jesus and wonder at his gracious words. Then they begin to doubt, asking, "Is not this Joseph's son?" Finally they put Jesus out of the city after he hints at the inclusion of the Gentiles within God's purpose of release from oppression and bondage. He gives the people two examples from the Old Testament to show that already centuries ago God was gracious to the Gentiles. When there was a great famine, Elijah was not sent to any of the widows in Israel, but only to a Phoenician widow. And Elisha healed none of the lepers in Israel, but only Naaman the Syrian.

What Jesus means is: because the Jews reject him as the fulfiller of Isaiah 61:1, he is now forced to offer salvation to the Gentiles, just as Elijah and Elisha did in their day. Already at the beginning of his public ministry, Jesus indicates that he has a mission to the Gentiles.

The Worldwide Gospel

The perspective of the gospel of Luke is more universal than that of Matthew and Mark. Luke sets his story in the context of world history. Jesus is born in Bethlehem because a decree has been issued by Caesar Augustus "that a census should be taken of the entire Roman world" (2:1). Jesus' genealogy is traced back to Adam (3:38), the forefather of all humankind, and not simply to his Jewish ancestors, David and Abraham, as is done in Matthew. The question of whether Jesus is sent only to the Jews is never raised in Luke, as it is in Matthew and Mark in the story of the Syro-Phoenician woman. And when Jesus is brought to trial, Luke's interest focuses on the proceedings in the Roman court, not, as in Matthew and Mark, on the proceedings in the Jewish court. Luke shows that Jesus' innocence was established before a Roman court—a world court. Three times (only once in Matthew and Mark) Pilate declares that Jesus is innocent of crime (23:4, 14-15, 22). It is only because the voices of the Jewish people prevail (23:23) that Pilate grants the option of choosing between Barabbas and Jesus.

Luke's worldwide perspective flows from his belief that Jesus' mission is worldwide. He begins his gospel with Simeon's announcement that the infant Jesus is "a light for revelation to the Gentiles" (2:32) and ends it with the risen Jesus reminding his disciples "that repentance and forgiveness of sins will be preached in his name to all nations" (24:47).

The Breakdown of Dividing Walls

In his gospel, Luke shows particular interest in Jesus' acceptance of people whom the Jews rejected from their society, people whom they held in contempt.

The Jews loathed tax collectors and classed them with robbers and murderers. These tax collectors willingly had contact with Gentiles and had a well-deserved reputation for dishonesty and extortion. Because of this the Jews excluded them from their society and excommunicated them from the synagogue.

The Jews despised the Samaritans, considering them racial and religious half-breeds. The Samaritans were descendants of Israelites and of Median and Persian colonists. These colonists had settled in the city of Samaria after it fell in 721 B.C., gradually abandoning their former pagan religion to become indistinguishable from the Israelites among whom they lived (see 2 Kings 17:24-34). The Samaritans recognized the Pentateuch as the Word of God and meticulously observed its precepts. But this did nothing to alter their exclusion from the Jewish community. The Jews continued to use the Samaritans' mixed racial origin as the expressed reason for refusing to have any dealings with them.

Luke relates the parable of the good Samaritan (10:25-37) and of the Pharisee and the tax collector (18:9-14). He records the story of Jesus' stay at the house of Zacchaeus the tax collector (19:1-10). And he tells us of the healing of the ten lepers and how only one of them—a Samaritan—returned to thank Jesus (17:11-19). Luke shows the kindness and gentleness of Jesus, but above all he shows that Jesus broke down barriers in preparation for the worldwide fellowship of humankind.

The Acts of the Apostles

Acts is the story of how Christianity traveled from Jerusalem to Rome. It records the transition of Christianity from a small group of Jewish disciples into a world religion. Luke traces this transition through six distinguishable stages:

The Church Is Born (Acts 1:2-6:7)

When the day of Pentecost arrives, God pours out his Spirit upon Jesus' followers. In his report of this event, Luke focuses on one effect: "All of them were filled with the Holy Spirit and began to speak in other tongues" (2:4). Luke also mentions a sound "like the blowing of a violent wind" (2:2) and "tongues of fire that separated and came to rest on each of them" (2:3), but these do not occupy his interest as does the speaking in tongues.

Luke does not explain the phenomenon of tongues. He sheds no light on how speaking with other tongues took place. All he says is that it took place. We are not told whether it was speaking in foreign languages or speaking in the language of the Spirit, whether it was a hearing miracle, a speaking miracle, or both. All Luke tells us is that at Pentecost the disciples praised God's mighty works in other tongues.

Pentecost envisions the proclamation of the gospel to "every nation under heaven" (2:5). When the Holy Spirit descends upon the disciples, they begin at once to address themselves to people of every nation and every tongue. The Spirit enables them to speak so that all their listeners understand. Pentecost, therefore, is the counterpart of Babel. It signals the restoration of the unity of humankind forfeited at Babel. At Babel, God "confused the language of the whole world" (Gen. 11:9). At Pentecost a new language is spoken, one that unites all peoples in spite of many linguistic and national barriers.

The outpouring of the Spirit, says Peter in his Pentecost sermon (2:14-36), marks the transition from the age of promise and preliminary fulfillment to the age of final fulfillment.

In Old Testament history, none of God's promises are finally fulfilled. From Abraham to Malachi, Israel constantly moves in the area of tension between God's promises and their provisional fulfillment. Israel lives by waiting.

The outpouring and activity of the Holy Spirit prove that the era of waiting is over and that the era of final fulfillment has arrived. "This is what was spoken by the prophet Joel: 'In the last days, God says, I will pour out my Spirit on all people' " (2:16-17). The age of final fulfillment has taken place through Jesus' death, resurrection, and ascension.

The Church Spreads Through Palestine (Acts 6:8-9:31)

The church of the early chapters of Acts is still entirely Jewish; all of its members are converted Jews. These Jewish Christians are of two kinds: the Hebrews—Aramaic-speaking Jews born in Palestine—and the Hellenists—Greek-speaking Diaspora Jews who have come to Jerusalem for a variety of reasons.

The earliest church only gradually left its Jewish cradle. For a while its members continued to attend the temple services and to uphold the precepts of the Torah.

Stephen, a Hellenistic Jew, is the first recorded Christian to launch an attack against both of these Jewish holdovers. He insists, first, that the temple is an obstacle in the way of God's march through history, and second, that the coming of Jesus profoundly changed the status of the Torah.

Stephen is arrested and brought before the Sanhedrin—the Jewish Supreme Court—because he blasphemed against the heart of Judaism: the Torah and the temple. In his defense speech (7:1-53) Stephen counters the charge as follows:

Concerning the Torah, Israel sins against the dynamic of its history when it declares the Torah to be God's *final* word. The history of Israel, from Abraham to Jesus, is a history kept in motion by God's promises and their preliminary fulfillments. It is a history that remains open to an unfulfilled future. The Torah is but a step towards the ultimate fulfillment of God's promises. Moses himself foretells the coming of a greater prophet (7:37). Therefore, believing that Jesus is the prophet promised by Moses constitutes loyalty, not disloyalty, to the Mosaic tradition.

Concerning the temple, Stephen reminds the Sanhedrin that God's first great revelations took place in foreign lands—in Ur, at Mt. Sinai, and in Midian—long before the temple existed (7:2-4, 29-34, 44-50) and that God's express orders were to build the tent of witness, not the temple (7:44). He argues that if the members of the Sanhedrin insist on stopping with Moses and the Torah, then, logically (since God did not give the temple plans to Moses), they should also stop with the tent of witness.

For espousing such views, Stephen is stoned to death. On the day of his death a great persecution arises against the church in Jerusalem. This persecution falls most heavily on the Hellenists, the group of which Stephen had been a leader. Philip, also a Hellenist, escapes to a city of Samaria and preaches Christ. As a result, many Samaritans believe.

The mass conversion of Samaritans marks a triumph of the Holy Spirit over a deep-seated national hatred between Jew and Samaritan. It also marks a strategic step towards Gentile mission, since racially the Samaritans are neither Jewish nor Gentile, but somewhere in between.

Philip's evangelistic activity also results in the conversion of an Ethiopian eunuch (8:26-40). Is this eunuch the first Gentile convert? The eunuch's religious status is not clearly stated. Is he a Jewish proselyte—someone who has accepted Judaism and has been circumcised? Is he a God-fearer— someone who is uncircumcised but attends the Jewish synagogue regularly and reads the Jewish Scriptures faithfully? Or is he a Gentile who has had no previous contact with Judaism?

Luke does not say. Perhaps his reason for not revealing the religious status of the eunuch is connected with the place of the story in the total context of Acts. The story is situated between the conversion of the Samaritans (8:4-25) and the conversion of the Gentiles (chapter 10). The screen of secrecy about the eunuch's religious status, writes Ernst Haenchen, "is best suited to the stage now reached in the history of the mission. Without permitting the emergence of all the problems which an explicit baptism of a Gentile must bring in its wake, Luke here leaves the reader with the feeling that with this new convert the mission has taken a step beyond the conversion of Jews and Samaritans. This eunuch will not be returning to Jerusalem, to place Christians in the embarrassment later provoked by the baptism of Cornelius" (*The Acts of the Apostles*, p. 314).

The Church Spreads to Syrian Antioch (Acts 9:32-12:24)

The first Gentile to join the church is a Roman centurion by the name of Cornelius. Cornelius is a God-fearer—someone who is attracted to the Jewish religion because of its monotheism and high morality, attends synagogue with some regularity, observes some of the Jewish practices, but has not been incorporated into the Jewish community by circumcision (10:2; 11:3). Through a heavenly vision God tells Peter to go to Cornelius and tell him about Jesus. In this vision Peter sees a great sheet full of clean and unclean animals. A voice commands: "Get up, Peter. Kill and eat." Peter replies: "Surely not, Lord! . . . for I have never eaten anything impure or unclean" (10:13f.).

Though Peter has been freed by Christ, he is still bound by the straitjacket of Jewish tradition. To him the Jewish tradition is the voice of God. But what he hears in the vision is also the voice of God. To which of these two voices should he listen?

Step by painful step, God leads him to obey the voice of the vision. Peter enters the home of Gentile Cornelius and preaches the gospel to him and his household. Then, following the outpouring of the Holy Spirit upon these "unclean" Gentiles, he commands that they be baptized without circumcision.

After Peter returns to Jerusalem, members of the "circumcision party" demand that he account for his actions. They believe that Gentiles can become Christians only if they have first been circumcised and keep the Torah food laws and purity regulations.

Peter justifies what he has done in these words: "If God gave them the same gift as he gave us, who believed in the Lord Jesus Christ, who was I to think that I could oppose God?" (11:17).

The problem plaguing Jewish Christians is whether the law of Moses retains its validity in the Christian church. What happens in Cornelius's home makes it clear, once and for all, that in order to become Christians, Gentiles do not have to become Jews first. By pouring out his Spirit on uncircumcised

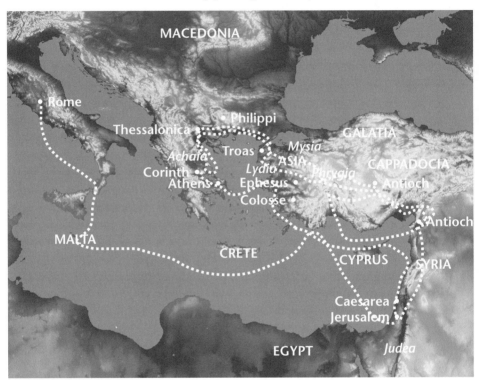

Paul's Missionary Journeys

Gentiles, God shows that the Gentile road to Christ does not pass through Judaism.

The problem of circumcision is officially solved at the Jerusalem Conference (chapter 15). This assembly adopts a resolution proposed by James. Gentile Christianity will be free from the Torah. Circumcision and all of its attendant legal obligations will not be imposed on Gentiles. Membership in the church will be by faith in Christ only.

The Church Spreads to Asia Minor (Acts 12:25-16:5)

At the time of Paul's conversion, the Lord said of him: "This man is my chosen instrument to carry my name before the Gentiles" (9:15). When a great number of Gentiles in Syrian Antioch turn to the Lord, the church in Jerusalem sends Barnabas to investigate. Barnabas wisely recognizes that the job of Gentile mission is too big for him to handle alone, and he therefore enlists the services of Paul. Paul not only has an in-depth knowledge of Judaism; he also knows the Roman and Greek world as few Jews do. Here, indeed, is a man prepared by God to be a bridge by which the Gentiles may come to know the God of Abraham, Isaac, and Jacob.

After Barnabas and Paul have worked in Syrian Antioch for a year (11:26), the Holy Spirit guides the church to release the two men for mission work in new areas. Paul and Barnabas first travel to Cyprus—Barnabas's native home. From there they set sail to the south coast of Asia Minor. They make their way to the city of Perga and from there, heading north, tramp over a third of Asia Minor until they come to Pisidian Antioch—the major military center of that part of the Roman province of Galatia.

Paul's message is enthusiastically received in the Antioch synagogue, especially by God-fearers. These converts spread the good news they have heard among their fellow Gentiles. So enthusiastic are their reports that a week later more Gentiles than Jews attend the synagogue service. This intrusion irks the Jews, and they openly contradict what Paul preaches. But many of the Gentiles accept the salvation that comes through faith in Jesus rather than through obedience to the Torah. They form a Christian congregation separate from the synagogue. "This is the moment of divorce between the gospel and Judaism" (Haenchen, *Acts,* p. 417).

Paul supports his decision to turn from the Jews to the Gentiles by quoting Isaiah 49:6, a passage which raises the question of the purpose of Israel's election. Why did God choose Israel? Not that it might enjoy special privileges, but that it might be "a light to the Gentiles"; that God's salvation might reach "to the ends of the earth" (Acts 13:47). If the Antioch Jews had accepted Paul's message that everyone who *believes* is justified (13:39), they would have had the honor of proclaiming God's salvation to their Gentile neighbors in fulfillment of Israel's world mission prophesied in Isaiah 49. But because they had refused to accept that God offers salvation to believing but uncircumcised Gentiles, Israel would be bypassed and the gospel offered to the Gentiles instead.

From Pisidian Antioch, Paul and Barnabas travel to Iconium, about ninety miles east-by-southeast; then to Lystra and Derbe. Later they retrace their steps, visiting and encouraging the members of the newly-founded churches in Lystra, Iconium, and Pisidian Antioch. Finally they return to Syrian Antioch and report to their sending church how God opened a door of faith to the Gentiles (14:27).

The Church Spreads to Macedonia and Greece (Acts 16:6-19:20)

Paul's aim is to win the Roman Empire for Christ. His strategy for doing this is to plant churches in the capital and major cities of each Roman province. The province of Galatia was his starting point for his first missionary journey.

On his second journey he plans to preach the gospel both in the western and northern parts of Asia Minor (16:6-8); Ephesus, the capital of the province of Asia, figures prominently in his plans. A strong church in that populous, gateway city between Asia and Europe would provide the route from Jerusalem to Rome with its last major station.

But the Holy Spirit twice thwarts Paul's plans, leading him across Asia Minor from the extreme southeast to the extreme northwest corner. There, in Troas, he finally receives a vision explaining the purpose of this strange journey. In this vision a man urges him to cross over to Macedonia and help the people there (16:9).

After seeing the vision, Paul immediately makes plans to sail to Macedonia. He lands in Neapolis (16:11) and from there travels inland to Philippi, where he gains his first European convert. From Philippi his travels lead him to Thessalonica, Berea, Athens, and Corinth; from Corinth he returns to the province of Asia, heading, at last, for its capital city, Ephesus.

During his stay at Ephesus, Paul engages in his most extensive missionary work. "All the Jews and Greeks who lived in the province of Asia heard the word of the Lord" (19:10). It is very likely that all seven churches mentioned in Revelation 2 and 3 are founded during this time, for they are all within easy reach of Ephesus and are all important trade centers.

The Church Spreads to Rome (Acts 19:21-28:29)

When Paul returns to Jerusalem after his second missionary journey, he says, "I must visit Rome also" (19:21). He does eventually visit Rome, but as a prisoner. For while in Jerusalem, he is arrested by Claudius Sergius, the Roman tribune. Because Paul is a Roman citizen and because the Jews are plotting to kill him, Sergius sends him at once to Felix, the Roman governor of Judea. In an explanatory letter Sergius states that Paul has done nothing to deserve prison or death under Roman law. Paul's conflict with the Jews, he notes, is purely a Jewish affair.

Though innocent under Roman law, Paul is not set free. Felix keeps Paul in custody for two years, to put himself in good standing with the Jews. Under Festus, Felix's successor, Paul appeals to Caesar (25:11). This appeal means that no one can convict or acquit him now except Caesar. Under military guard, Paul now travels to Rome, where for two years "boldly and without hindrance he preached the kingdom of God and taught about the Lord Jesus Christ" (28:31).

It is deeply significant that the words "without hindrance" should be included, for the road from Jerusalem to Rome has been one long obstacle course. In 2 Corinthians 11:23-27 Paul recites some of these obstacles:

> I have served more prison sentences! I have been beaten times without number. I have faced death again and again. I have been beaten the regulation thirty-nine stripes by the Jews five times. I have been beaten with rods three times. I have been stoned once. I have been shipwrecked

three times. I have been twenty-four hours in the open sea. In my travels I have been in constant danger from rivers and floods, from bandits, from my own countrymen, and from pagans. I have faced danger in city streets, danger in the desert, danger on the high seas, danger among false Christians. I have known exhaustion, pain, long vigils, hunger and thirst, doing without meals, cold and lacking of clothing (Phillips).

Another important word in the final chapter of Acts is the word "Jews." Luke's two-volume work, the gospel of Luke and the Acts of the Apostles, is bracketed by two Jewish rejections of the gospel. In Luke 4:29, the Nazareth Jews are ready to lynch Jesus. In Acts 28:24, Roman Jews reject Paul's exposition of the gospel, so that Paul sees the prophecy of Isaiah 6:9-10 fulfilled: the Jews have hardened their hearts; salvation is now for the Gentiles. And the Gentiles will listen.

Why, after arriving in Rome, does Paul bother with the Jews at all? Why does he contact them first? Paul's main reason is his conviction that because salvation is from the Jews, the gospel should always first be offered to them.

One of the biggest problems facing the early church was the refusal by the great majority of Jews to confess Jesus as the promised Messiah. Though the church was built upon Israel, Israel as a whole refused to enter the church. Nevertheless, Israel remains the people of God's first call, "for God's gifts and his call are irrevocable" (Rom. 11:29). The God of the church is the God of Israel, whose plan for Israel is unchanged.

Nine: God Gathers All His People

Chapter Review Questions

1. Luke 4:28 says that the people of Nazareth "were furious" with Jesus. Why were they so angry?

2. What is Luke's purpose in telling the parable of the good Samaritan and the story of Zacchaeus?

3. What is the significance of Pentecost (Acts 2)?

4. What is revolutionary about Stephen's speech before the Sanhedrin (Acts 7:1-53)?

5. After consulting the map on page 112 of the text, ask yourself: Why does Paul travel the way he does? What plan dictates his journeys?

6. Why is Ephesus so important to Paul?

General Discussion Questions

1. Why was Pentecost necessary? Hadn't God already given his Spirit to his people in the Old Testament?

2. Christians regularly want to go back to the type of Christianity described in the book of Acts. Is this in fact the purest form of Christianity?

3. Why is the story of Cornelius (Acts 10) a turning point in the history of the early church?

4. What danger lurks behind the triumphal picture of the church painted in Acts?

5. Why do you think the book of Acts ends so abruptly?

Notes

Ten: God Reconstitutes His People

The Old Testament tells how God chose a people—Israel—to be the agent of his plan for the world. For twenty centuries God instructed and disciplined this people so that they could bear witness to his redeeming love for the world. "I will also make you a light for the Gentiles, that you may bring my salvation to the ends of the earth" (Isa. 49:6).

God spent twenty centuries forming the people from whom his Son was to be born. Yet it took this people only three years to turn against God's Son and kill him. The rejection of Jesus by the Jewish people: how could it have happened? No one has pondered this question more deeply than the apostle Paul.

The New People of God

God chose Israel to be his instrument—through Israel his salvation would reach all nations (Gen. 12:3; 18:18). All God's preparations for the Christ took place within this nation.

Out of Egypt God called Israel, his son (Hos. 11:1). His glory went before them in the pillars of cloud and fire (Ex. 13:21). God bound himself to them by covenants and promises. He gave them the law and the temple worship. He raised up Jesus the Messiah from among them. To this nation, says Paul, belongs "adoption as sons, the divine glory, the covenants, the receiving of the law, the temple worship and the promises. Theirs are the patriarchs, and from them is traced the human ancestry of Christ" (Rom. 9:4-5).

Nevertheless, Israel rejected Jesus and so apparently excluded itself from the salvation offered in him. This rejection causes Paul great sorrow and unceasing anguish and he wishes that, in their stead, he "were cursed and cut off from Christ" (Rom. 9:3).

When Jesus came to his people, why didn't they receive him? When Jesus proclaimed, "The time has come. . . . The kingdom of God is near" (Mark 1:15), why didn't Israel know the fullness of its own history? Does Israel's rejection of Jesus mean God's rejection of Israel? Does Israel now drop out of God's plan, or is its rejection of Jesus part of God's plan?

Not for a moment will Paul consider the possibility that God is through with Israel. Throughout the two thousand years of Israel's history, God had never completely rejected his people. Why then would he do so now? The entire Old Testament is one continuous refutation of this possibility. The Old Testament prophets consistently claim that Israel is destined to play a central role in the redemption of the world at the end of time.

Israel's rejection of Jesus, Paul claims, is to open the way for the Gentiles to come into the kingdom of God. Because the Jews refuse to believe, the gospel goes to the Gentiles who are eager to listen. Israel's rejection enriches the entire world. Without being aware of it, Israel is again the instrument of God's action in history, the agent of world-wide redemption.

If Israel's rejection of the gospel enriches the world by opening the door to the Gentiles, can you imagine what Israel's acceptance will mean? "For if their rejection is the reconciliation of the world, what will their acceptance be but life from the dead?" (Rom. 11:15). Israel is fighting its age-long battle with God, but God's pursuing love still follows Israel. And God's love will continue to follow until both Jews and Gentiles are gathered into the one people of God.

God's plan is that Jews *and* Gentiles shall constitute his people. This plan was conceived by the Father and hidden in him from all eternity (Eph. 3:9). Christ revealed this divine plan to the world. He put it into effect by breaking down the dividing wall of hostility between Jews and Gentiles so that both can be members of the same people, the new Israel (Eph. 2:14-16). Just as the Gentiles were once disobedient to God but now have received mercy, so the Jews are now temporarily disobedient in order that by the mercy shown to them they also may receive mercy. "For God has bound all men over to disobedience so that he may have mercy on them all" (Rom. 11:32).

Paul's Argument with the Jews

Paul's basic argument with the Jews of his day is about the righteousness from God. In Philippians 3:4-9 he contrasts this righteousness from God with righteousness under the Jewish law:

> If anyone else thinks he has reason to put confidence in the flesh, I have more: circumcised on the eighth day, of the people of Israel, of the tribe of Benjamin, a Hebrew of Hebrews; in regard to the law, a Pharisee; as for zeal, persecuting the church; as for legalistic righteousness, faultless. But whatever was to my profit, I now consider loss for the sake of Christ. What is more, I consider everything a loss compared to the surpassing greatness of knowing Christ Jesus my Lord, for whose sake I have lost all things. I consider them rubbish, that I may gain Christ and be found in him, not having a righteousness of my own that comes from the law, but that which is through faith in Christ—the righteousness that comes from God and is by faith.

In this passage, Paul exemplifies the merchant in Jesus' parable who was in search of fine pearls and, on finding one pearl of great value, went and sold all that he had and bought it (Matt. 13:45-46).

Paul lists the "fine pearls" that he now considers to be worthless: he is
circumcised, which proves that his parents were not Gentiles; he is not a

proselyte, but of direct Israelite descent; he belongs, not to a renegade tribe, but to the faithful tribe of Benjamin; he belongs to a Dispersion family that has not adopted the language and conformed to the customs of the people around them, but has maintained the Hebrew language and Hebrew customs; he belongs to a sect that most strictly observes the Jewish law; and he has left nothing undone which the law requires.

This collection of pearls, Paul has discovered, cannot make him acceptable to God. His pursuit of "a righteousness . . . that comes from the law" (Phil. 3:9) did not lead into the presence of God.

Over against Judaism, which summons people to work out their own salvation, Paul places the gospel, which claims that Christ has fulfilled all the requirements of the law for us and that, if we believe in Christ, we receive righteousness from God as a free gift.

First-century Judaism was the noblest religion in the ancient world. The Pharisaic sect—to which Paul belonged—represented its most earnest and progressive development. This noble religion, however, bred a self-righteousness that prevented people from hearing God's radical call—to repent and believe the gospel. In their self-righteousness, the Jews considered themselves to be on the side of God, but exempt from repentance and belief in the gospel. Because they saw themselves as already righteous under the law, they were blinded to their need for the righteousness from God, which is through faith in Christ.

The Jews could not see how God could have sent his Messiah to tax collectors and to people ignorant of the law. The Messiah would most certainly appear among the righteous—those who by their zealous observance of the law were standing on the side of God.

Then, on the road to Damascus, Paul met the Messiah who had eaten with tax collectors and sinners, with morally and spiritually bankrupt people, and his eyes were opened to see "the righteousness that comes from God and is by faith." After this encounter the central fact of his life was that God had found and accepted him while he was yet a sinner.

Joining the New People of God

The church is the new people of God. How does a person become part of God's new people? By baptism. But why is baptism the gateway to God's new people? Paul answers this question in Romans 6:1-11.

Baptism, Paul explains, signifies a dying with Christ and a rising with Christ. It means a dying of the old self with Christ and a rising of the new self with Christ. "Don't you know that all of us who were baptized into Christ Jesus were baptized into his death? We were therefore buried with him through baptism into death in order that, just as Christ was raised from the dead through the glory of the Father, we too may live a new life" (Rom. 6:3-4).

To understand this kind of language, it is helpful to know how most early Christians were baptized. There were four specific acts in the baptismal ceremony.   121

First, the candidates for baptism took off their clothes, as a sign of putting off the old nature, which belonged to their "former way of life" and was "corrupted by its deceitful desires" (Eph. 4:22).

Next, they went down into the baptismal water and, one by one, were submerged. This symbolized their dying and being buried with Christ (Col. 2:12).

Then they came up. This rising from the baptismal water symbolized their rising with Christ to a new life.

After coming out of the water, the newly baptized Christians put on fresh clothing—a symbol of their putting on "the new self created to be like God in true righteousness and holiness" (Eph. 4:24).

Being baptized means entering into the redemptive acts of Christ's life. In baptism Christians reenact in their own lives the two basic events of Christ's life: his death and his resurrection. These cease to be merely events that occurred in the past; they begin to exert a powerful influence on the Christian's daily living. "As Christ died to break the destructive reign of sin over man, the believer dies with him to sin and to his old sinful self; and as Christ rose from the dead to open to men a new age of grace, the believer rises with him into a new life of grace and of the Spirit" (James D. Smart, *Doorway to a New Age,* p. 87).

How does one join the new people of God? Not by self-improvement. Christ did not come into the world to make us better. He did not come into the world to improve us, but to make us into new creatures altogether.

This explanation of baptism throws light on Paul's favorite phrase, "in Christ." As a Jew, Paul had been "in Israel"; he had identified himself with the history of Israel. For the true Jew "is one who has so entered the history of his people that that history has become his own history, just as the true American is one who has, in his own experience, crossed the Atlantic with the pilgrim fathers, wrestled with the wilderness of early America, fought the War of Independence and the Civil War, and sat down at the table with Washington, Jefferson, Lincoln, and Lee. To be 'in Israel' meant to recapture and reenact the experiences of the people of Israel, to make its history living, contemporary history" (W. D. Davies, *The New Creation,* p. 7f.).

Following his conversion, Paul, though he does not cease to think of himself as a Jew, is a member of a people who derive their life solely from Christ. To be "in Christ" means to be a living member of this people. Just as being "in Israel" means to appropriate to one's self the history of the people of Israel, so to be "in Christ" means to appropriate to one's self the history of Christ, particularly his death and resurrection.

Preparation for Joining the New People of God

Converts coming out of Judaism or out of paganism needed moral guidance. Not only were they instructed in the words and works of Jesus but also, before being baptized, they received specific instructions in the moral implications of their baptismal participation in Jesus' death and resurrection.

In his book *Paul and Rabbinic Judaism,* W. D. Davies cites a number of passages from New Testament letters that in all likelihood were used for pre-baptismal ethical instruction. These passages show a remarkable similarity both in content and in order, and are best explained as material used by the early church for instructing candidates for baptism. It seems that there was a common body of catechetical material for baptism, probably oral, that Paul and other New Testament writers used.

The following six tables reveal the pattern of pre-baptismal instruction. Converts to the Christian faith were told to

1. Put off the old self

Colossians 3:8-9: "you have taken off your old self with its practices"
Ephesians 4:22, 25–5:17: "put off your old self"
1 Peter 2:1: "rid yourself of all malice: and all deceit, hypocrisy"
James 1:21: "get rid of all moral filth"

2. Put on the new self

Colossians 3:10-15: "put on the new self"
Ephesians 4:23-24: "put on the new self"
1 Peter 1:22-23: "love one another. . . . you have been born again"
James 1:18: "be a kind of firstfruits of all he created"

3. Worship God

Colossians 3:16-17: "giving thanks to God the Father through him [Jesus Christ]"
Ephesians 5:18-20: "giving thanks to God the Father"
1 Peter 2:5: "offering spiritual sacrifices acceptable to God"
James 1:26-27: "religion that God our Father accepts as pure and faultless"

4. Submit themselves

Colossians 3:18-22: "Wives, submit to your husbands. . . . Husbands, love your wives. . . . Children, obey your parents. . . . Fathers, do not embitter your children. . . . Slaves, obey"
Ephesians 5:21–6:9: "submit to one another. . . . Wives. . . . Husbands. . . . Children. . . . Fathers. . . . Slaves. . . . Masters"
1 Peter 2:13–3:7: "submit . . . to every authority instituted among men. . . . Slaves. . . . Wives. . . . Husbands"
James 4:7: "Submit yourselves, then, to God"

5. Watch and pray

Colossians 4:2-6: "Devote yourselves to prayer, being watchful"
Ephesians 6:18: "pray . . . on all occasions. . . . be alert"
1 Peter 4:7: "be clear minded and self-controlled so that you can pray"

6. Stand and resist the devil

Colossians 4:12: "stand firm"
Ephesians 6:10-17: "stand against the devil's schemes"
1 Peter 5:8-12: "resist him"
James 4:7: "resist the devil"

The New Morality

Implied in Baptism

The Israelites in the wilderness "all were baptized into Moses in the cloud and in the sea" (1 Cor. 10:2). And yet, so Paul reminds his Corinthians converts, God was not pleased with most of them and sentenced them to perish in the wilderness.

What Paul means is this: baptism—into Moses or into Christ—achieves nothing unless it is an outward symbol of an inward change. Baptism is not a magical rite. It does not operate automatically. Baptismal water does not automatically preserve the Christian until death. No, it is a water in which the old self drowns and from which the new self rises. The test of a person's baptism is the moral quality of his or her life. Those who have been baptized must consider themselves "dead to sin but alive to God in Christ Jesus" (Rom. 6:11). Baptism, which signifies a dying and rising with Christ, must manifest itself in a new moral lifestyle.

But apparently the moral revolution never took place in the lives of many of Paul's converts. Paul, therefore, repeatedly urges them to live their baptism, to put off the old self and put on the new self "created to be like God" (Eph. 4:24). He exhorts these young Christians: "No longer live as the Gentiles do" (Eph. 4:17), for once you were darkness but now you are light in the Lord. You should, therefore, walk as children of light (Eph. 5:8). Once you were hostile to God, doing evil deeds; now you are reconciled to him (Col. 1:21-22). Once you were dead in trespasses; now you are alive together with Christ (Col. 2:13). You must, therefore, put to death what belongs to your old self, and put on the new self (Col. 3:8-9).

Certain things made it easy for these early Christians to ignore the moral implications of their baptism. For example, they lived in the burning hope of Christ's imminent return from heaven and for that reason were easily tempted to focus all their attention on the future and to neglect or slight the present. In his first letter to the Thessalonians, Paul warns against this particular danger. He urges his readers to keep the highest moral standards in sexual and family life (4:1-8) and to continue in mutual love and daily work (4:9-12).

Prompted by the Holy Spirit

Through his resurrection Christ became "a life-giving spirit" (1 Cor. 15:45). The Spirit God sends to live in his people is the Spirit of his Son: "Because you are sons, God sent the Spirit of his Son into our hearts" (Gal. 4:6). For this reason anyone who is "in Christ" can also be described as being "in the Spirit"; "You . . . are controlled . . . by the Spirit, if the Spirit of God lives in you. And if anyone does not have the Spirit of Christ, he does not belong to Christ. But if Christ is in you, your body is dead because of sin, yet your spirit is alive because of righteousness" (Rom. 8:9-10).

Or, to put it another way: the Holy Spirit, living in believers, produces in their lives the qualities of Jesus' life. The Holy Spirit is the Spirit of Christ-likeness. The fruits of the Spirit—love, joy, peace, patience, kindness, goodness, faithfulness, gentleness, self-control—describe the character of Jesus. It is the work of the Spirit to progressively actualize in us the character of Jesus.

The true source of Christian behavior is the indwelling Spirit of the risen Christ. When faced with a moral choice, mature Christians do not ask, Would I disappoint myself, or my community? but, Would I grieve the Holy Spirit who lives within me? The Spirit of the risen Christ becomes the judge of moral behavior.

The presence of the Spirit sharpens rather than weakens moral sensitivity, for "the moral demand of letting Christ's Spirit rule in you in everything is far more searching than the demand of any code, and at the same time it carries with it the promise of indefinite growth and development. It means that every Christian is a centre of fermentation where the morally revolutionary Spirit of Christ attacks the dead mass of the world. Ethical originality is the prerogative of the Christian whose conscience is the seat of Christ's indwelling" (C. H. Dodd, *The Meaning of Paul for Today*, p. 147).

Upbuilding the People of God

The Holy Spirit, besides being the source of Christian morality, is also the creator of Christian unity. The life of both the new person and the new Israel flow from the Spirit. Christians as individuals but also as a body constitute a temple of the Holy Spirit. In consonance with this, gifts of the Spirit are bestowed, not for individual self-gratification, but for the upbuilding of the entire people of God.

There is one basic gift that all believers receive from God—the Holy Spirit. But this one gift manifests itself in the lives of Christians in a variety of ways. Like a ray of sunlight passing through a prism and refracting into a spectrum of colors, so the Holy Spirit manifests its life in the church through a variety of gifts.

These gifts include abilities not widely possessed before the outpouring of the Spirit, such as gifts of prophecy, healing, or speaking in tongues, and also the heightening of qualities already present, such as gifts of teaching, organizing, or exhorting.

All these gifts, acquired or inherent, are to be dedicated to the service of God and the church. If they are used selfishly, they can be destructive. Depending on whether they are used "for the common good" (1 Cor. 12:7) or for self-gratification, these gifts can be a blessing or a curse. Here the Christian must be on the alert. Next to the genuine there frequently appears the counterfeit. Thus, for example, speaking in tongues is found not only in Christianity but also in other religions. Jesus warned his disciples to that effect when he told them that signs and wonders would be performed also by the false Christs and false prophets (Mark 13:22; Matt. 24:24). Having the power to perform signs and wonders means little by itself. The power must be enlisted in the service of Christ if it is to bear the sample of divine authorship. Apart from Christ such gifts can lead to pride and divisiveness. For this reason 1 Corinthians 13 appears right in the middle of Paul's discussion of gifts. A person may be richly endowed with gifts, but resembles "a resounding gong or a clanging cymbal" (v. 1) if that supreme gift of the Spirit—love—is lacking. As for prophecies, they will pass. As for tongues and healings, they will cease. Only love is stronger than death and lasts forever.

Ten: God Reconstitutes His People

Chapter Review Questions

1. How does Paul account for the mystery of the Jewish rejection of Jesus?

2. Paul's basic argument with the Jews of his day has to do with the righteousness from God. How would you reformulate that argument for the people of our day?

3. What, according to Romans 6:1-11, is Paul's view of baptism?

4. What are the moral implications of baptism?

5. How does the Holy Spirit build Christian unity? See 1 Corinthians 12:1-20.

General Discussion Questions

1. What if God were to be unfaithful to the promise he made to Israel in Jeremiah 31:37? What if God were to reject Israel? Where would that leave us, Gentile Christians?

2. How has the Holocaust forced the church to take a fresh look at Romans 9-11?

3. What does Paul mean by being justified through faith (Rom. 5:1-11)?

4. First Corinthians 15 is considered one of the most important sections in Paul's letters. Why is it so central to our faith?

Notes

Eleven: God Reveals the Interior of History

Picture a beautiful sunset. Watching it are a poet, a musician, and a painter. After the sun has set, all return home and translate the experience into the language of their artistic medium. The poet writes a poem. The musician composes a piece of music. The painter projects what he saw onto a piece of canvas. Objectively speaking, the sunset was the same for all three. Yet each gives different artistic expression to it.

The same is true of Jesus' ministry. Objectively speaking, his ministry is the same for all. Yet how different are the ways in which the early Christians gave literary expression to what they heard and saw. They told about Jesus' ministry in historical narrative: "In those days Caesar Augustus issued a decree that a census should be taken of the entire Roman world" (Luke 2:1). Or they sang about it in hymns: "[Christ] appeared in a body, was indicated by the Spirit, was seen by angels, was preached among the nations, was believed on in the world, was taken up in glory" (1 Tim. 3:16). Or they confessed it in creedal form: We believe "that Christ died for our sins according to the Scriptures, that he was buried, that he was raised on the third day according to the Scriptures, and that he appeared to Peter, and then to the Twelve" (1 Cor. 15:3-5). Or they translated it into the strange imagery and symbolism of apocalyptic language—language that abounds in heavenly visions filled with bizarre creatures out of which the modern reader can make neither head nor tail.

What Is Apocalyptic Literature?

The term *apocalyptic* is derived from a Greek word that means "unveiling." Apocalyptic literature claims to unveil events that will take place in the end time, when this world will end and the kingdom of God will be ushered in. Literature of this kind flourished in the Jewish world between the second century B.C. and the first century A.D. In his book *The Relevance of Apocalyptic,* H. H. Rowley lists the following apocalyptic writings of Jewish and Christian origin produced in his period:

The Book of Daniel
The Ethiopic Book of Enoch (1 Enoch)
The Book of Jubilees
Testaments of the Twelve Patriarchs

The Sibylline Oracles
The Psalms of Solomon
The Zadokite Work
The Qumran Scrolls
The Assumption of Moses
The Slavonic Book of Enoch (2 Enoch)
The Life of Adam and Eve
4 Ezra (2 Esdras)
The Apocalypse of Baruch
The Ascension of Isaiah
The Apocalypse of Abraham
The Testament of Abraham
The Little Apocalypse of the Gospels (Mark 13)
The Book of Revelation

Apocalyptic writings were created in times of desperate need and sprang from a desire to minister to those needs. They tried to explain why the righteous suffered and why the kingdom of God was delayed.

What characterizes these writings is their exclusive occupation with the future. Apocalyptists believed that the evils at work in the world are beyond human sin or human repentance. Demonic in nature and cosmic in scope, these evils can be overcome only by direct divine intervention. They saw the events of their day as signs that the cosmic struggle between God and the powers of evil was moving to its climax. The present age was hurrying to the end. The new age, the transformation of all things, was at hand.

True apocalyptists, writes Leon Morris, foresaw "the final breaking up of everything that is familiar, the destruction of a whole way of life, even of a whole universe" (*Apocalyptic,* p. 41). In this they differed basically from Old Testament prophets. Though prophets were concerned with the future, they always immersed themselves in the contemporary crisis. In contrast, the supreme interest of apocalyptists was in the grand finale of history and in the time of unprecedented suffering immediately preceding it.

Is the Book of Revelation Apocalyptic Literature?

The book of Revelation is generally classified as an example of apocalyptic writing. One can easily see why. The language is heavenly and cosmic rather than historical and political. And the actors (Son of man, Satan, angels, a heavenly woman) and the properties (new Jerusalem, the heavenly temple, the throne of God, the stars, the bottomless pit) are supernatural.

There are, however, certain elements that do not fit the apocalyptic pattern. First, the writer calls this book a prophecy, not just once but repeatedly. In the opening chapter he writes: "Blessed is the one who reads the words of this prophecy" (v. 3). And in the closing chapter he writes: "Blessed is he who keeps the words of the prophecy in this book" (v. 7; see also v. 10, 18, 19). Thus the book is bracketed between two beatitudes that specifically state that its contents are prophetic.

Second, apocalypses usually were written under a pseudonym; the book of Revelation is not. Apocalyptists did not write in their own name but under an assumed name—that of an outstanding person of antiquity. They did this to lend an authoritative ring to what they wrote. John, on the other hand, wrote in his own name, in the conviction that what he wrote had the authority of the living Christ behind it.

Third, apocalyptists were concerned with comforting and encouraging the persecuted people of God, whereas prophets confronted the people to whom they had been sent with a demand for repentance. The book of Revelation does exclusively neither the one nor the other. It does both. It is prophetic—preaching repentance and judgment to the entire church; it is apocalyptic—offering comfort and encouragement to the persecuted people of God.

Fourth, John's interpretation of history differs radically from that of the apocalyptists of that era. The typical apocalyptist was extremely pessimistic about the age, seeing it as completely dominated by evil forces. John sees his age through different eyes. He sees the interior of history—history as invaded and conquered by Jesus Christ, who now, through the power of his resurrection, makes all things new. That's why John's book is called Apocalypse; it unveils the rule of Christ still hidden behind the ugly shape of historical events.

There are more differences between Revelation and apocalyptic writings, but these four are sufficient to show that although John's work has some affinity with them, essentially it is quite different, especially in the way it interprets history. The book of Revelation "is a Christian writing setting forth what God has done in Christ and what He will yet do, and using something of the apocalyptic method to bring all this out. But the emphasis on 'the Lamb as it had been slain,' i.e., on a past event of history, is both central to Revelation and absent from the apocalypses" (Morris, *Apocalyptic,* p. 81).

The Lamb That Was Slain

The apocalyptists present two subsequent periods of time: the present age and then, immediately following, the new age. But John, as we have seen, presents the new age as having already invaded the present age. John does not look away from history but looks at history with new eyes. In its interior he discerns the kingly rule of Christ. The central message of his book is: Jesus' death and resurrection have brought in the new age.

The book of Revelation portrays Christ, seated at the right hand of God, exercising his kingly power. It does not map out the course of history. By reading it, no one will be able to predict what events are going to take place. It does not reveal the *course* of history but the *depth* of history. It presents a vision of the kingly power of Christ being exercised in the midst of history.

After John has finished the messages to the seven churches in Asia Minor (chapters 2-3), he begins to write about his interpretation of history—history centered in Christ. He sees an open door in heaven and hears a voice that invites him to witness a liturgy in which the whole court of heaven sings praise to God:

You are worthy, our Lord and God,
to receive glory and honor and power,
for you created all things,
and by your will they were created and have their being (4:11).

Then the glorified Christ appears. He is introduced as the Lion of the tribe of Judah, the Root of David, who "has triumphed. He is able to open the scroll and its seven seals" (5:5). From the right hand of God, Christ then takes the sealed scroll, which no one in heaven or on earth is able to open or to look into. On the scroll is written God's plan for creation and history.

Because Christ has conquered, it is in his power to open the great book of history. And the heavenly chorus affirms this:

You are worthy to take the scroll and to open its seals,
because you were slain and with your blood you purchased men for God
from every tribe and language and people and nation.
You have made them to be a kingdom and priests to serve our God,
and they will reign on the earth (5:9-10).

This is John's way of expressing Christ's ascension into heaven. Having gained victory over Satan through his death and resurrection, Christ, the sacrificial Lamb, enters the heavenly council and receives power from the right hand of God. Because he was slain, he is worthy to open the scroll of history both to reveal and carry out the final dissolution of all powers that oppose the rule of God.

Christ, John is saying, is the key that unlocks the meaning of history. History permits two different readings: a superficial and an in-depth reading. The one denies Christ's rule; the other affirms that the kingly rule of Christ has already broken into our world and is already at work among us. Because this rule is concealed behind the forms and events of this world, we are unable to see it directly. We cannot trace the course of the kingdom of God by tracing the course of history. But to the eye of faith it is a fact that God presently governs the course of the world, that Christ presently is holding the scroll of history in his hands. The eye of faith discerns the innermost secret of history: the judgment that would have fallen on humanity and on the world has, instead, fallen on Jesus. The type of calamities described in Revelation are the judgments of God upon history "which *would have had to be,* if man had been left to himself, if God had judged this history and man in themselves" (Jacques Ellul, *Apocalypse,* p. 146).

Apocalyptists believed that the new age would first come at the close of the present age. John believed that the coming of Christ inaugurated the new age. So, the two ages overlap and interact. To the present age belong all "whose names have not been written in the book of life belonging to the Lamb that was slain from the creation of the world" (13:8). To the new age belong all creatures "in heaven and on earth and under the earth and on the sea" (5:13) who worship God and the Lamb. For the time being people belonging to these different ages work together, do business together, and even marry. Yet they do not live in the same age. The ultimate loyalty of the one group is to the beast; that of the other, to the Lamb that was slain.

The Law of Sevens

A quick glance at the outline of the book of Revelation as offered by Hanns Lilje shows that the number seven is basic to its structure:

> The sevenfold exhortation (2:1-3:22)
> The sevenfold prophecy (4:1-5:14)
> The seven seals (6:1-7:17)
> The seventh seal: the seven trumpets (8:1-11:14)
> The seventh trumpet: the seven dragon visions (11:14-13:18)
> The seven visions of the Son of man (14:1-20)
> The seven bowls of the wrath of God (15:1-16:21)
> The seven visions of the fall of Babylon (17:1-19:10)
> The seven visions of fulfillment (19:11-21:5a)

Behind this use of the sacred number seven is the conviction that nothing in history happens by chance, that everything takes place within the confines of a divine plan. "All events, even the most terrible, are under the control of a holy order; everything takes place in accordance with an eternal plan. Thus there are gleams of divine order shining through the stormy clouds of eschatological terror. The Christian who gazes at this drama of the end of history should not be disturbed by any doubt or anxiety, because he sees behind it all the hand of God ordering all things according to his will" (Hanns Lilje, *The Last Book of the Bible,* p. 28).

The Defeat of the Dragon

Chapter 12 is one of the most important chapters in the book of Revelation. As the chapter begins, a pregnant woman clothed with the sun and with the moon under her feet and on her head a crown of twelve stars cries out in the pain of bringing forth her child. The woman's cry, which echoes through the heavens, is mingled with the joy of anticipation: something new is about to take place, a male child "who will rule all the nations with an iron scepter" (12:5) is about to be born.

To understand this vision, we must avoid the mistake of expecting the book of Revelation to say something different from what the gospels are saying. In Revelation we must be prepared to hear the same message we hear in the gospels—only, in Revelation the message is conveyed through the peculiar medium of apocalyptic images and symbols.

Thus, Revelation 12:1-5 is an apocalyptic expression of the Christmas story: the pregnant woman is Israel and the child about to be born is Jesus. The gospel of Luke, too, describes the birth of Jesus, but in the language of historical narrative. Luke narrates the birth of Jesus as an event that took place in a forgotten corner of the Roman Empire and in the greatest secrecy. Revelation 12, in typical apocalyptic fashion, projects the story of Jesus' birth on a cosmic screen so that the whole world can see it. In Revelation 12, Jesus' birth is a public, a cosmic, event. What once happened in a hidden corner is here reenacted before the eyes of the whole world, so that no one can plead ignorance of it.

John also portrays Jesus' ascension apocalyptically. In Luke's gospel Jesus ascends to heaven from Bethany, a small, insignificant village. Only his disciples are watching. In Revelation 12:5 Jesus is caught up to God and to his throne before the whole world. His lordship is manifested to all.

John also translates Jesus' temptations into apocalyptic language. The way the gospels tell the story, Satan's temptations of Jesus took place in the wilderness—the most out-of-sight place in the world—with no one present except wild beasts and angels (Mark 1:13). The way John tells the story, a great red dragon whose tail sweeps over the heaven and causes a third of the stars to fall upon the earth stands before the woman "that he might devour her child the moment it was born" (12:4). If Jesus had yielded to the dragon's temptations, if he had commanded stones to become loaves of bread, if he had thrown himself down from the temple, and if he had fallen down and worshiped his opponent, he would have forfeited the throne of the world. But he withstood the temptations and therefore "was snatched up to God and to his throne" (12:5). His ascension seals the defeat of the dragon, "that ancient serpent called the devil, or Satan, who leads the whole world astray" (12:9), and Satan is thrown out of heaven. This calls for a song of victory:

> Now have come the salvation and the power
> and the kingdom of our God,
>   and the authority of his Christ.
> For the accuser of our brothers,
> who accuses them before our God day and night, has been hurled down.
> They overcame him by
> the blood of the Lamb
>   and by their word of their testimony;
> they did not love their lives so much as to shrink from death.
> Therefore rejoice, you heavens and you who dwell in them! (12:10-12).

The decisive battle has been won. The dragon has been utterly defeated. But because of that, the earth is thrown into a turmoil. All the powers of evil, dislodged by Christ, now fall upon the earth, upon the followers of Christ. Will they be engulfed by this outbreak of evil? No! says John. They overcome it "by the blood of the Lamb and by the word of their testimony" (12:11). Who shall separate them from the love of Christ? Shall tribulation or distress or persecution? No, in all these things they are more than conquerors through him who loves them.

The Message of the Millennium

Few chapters in the Bible have generated such heated discussion as Revelation 20. How are we to interpret it? One guideline is clear: like the rest of the book, this chapter must be read in the light of Christ's assumption of world power and of his decisive victory over Satan.

Revelation 20 allows for two basic interpretations. It can be interpreted literally, or it can be interpreted literarily, that is, in accordance with the kind of literature that the book of Revelation represents.

Those who interpret this chapter literally say it is a prediction of what is actually going to happen, and exactly as described. They say that a thousand years of earthly utopia—a so-called millennium—will be introduced by the resurrection of a small section of humanity, of those who have "not worshiped the beast or his image" (20:4). A rule of peace and justice will be established within the historical world. It will last for a thousand years—years measured by our earthly calendar.

The basic weakness of this interpretation is that it lifts this chapter out of its apocalyptic framework and brings it down to the plane of human history. We need to remind ourselves, however, that we are dealing with a vision that is couched in apocalyptic imagery and symbolism. Furthermore, to interpret Revelation 20 literally means going against the very purpose of the book of Revelation, which is to make us see the new age, not at the end of the present age, but in the very middle of it. Its purpose is to reveal the eternal in time, the action of the end in the present, the kingly rule of Christ in the interior of human history. In view of this, writes Thomas F. Torrance, "we have no more right to take this thousand years literally than we have to take the ten-headed and seven-horned monster literally. It is entirely out of place . . . to bring down the thousand years out of its apocalyptic setting and place it on the ordinary plane of history, as if it could be handled by a worldly arithmetic and manipulated in calculations about the dispensations of time or about the end of the world" (*The Apocalypse Today*, p. 162f.).

When we interpret Revelation 20 literarily, that is, when we recognize its distinctive literary character, we see the thousand years not as a span of time that can be measured against the clock but as an apocalyptic expression for the fullness of time (10x10x10) that has broken into our world through the death and resurrection of Jesus Christ. The thousand years represents kingdom time—time that is full because in it God exercises full control. This kingdom time has already broken into our world. Millennium time is *now*. It is the time of Jesus Christ. It is the time in which the ascended Christ is working hard at setting the whole creation free from bondage. It is history viewed from the perspective of the enthroned Christ, who secretly and mysteriously is making all world events serve the purpose of God.

Many Christians are sky gazers. Like the apocalyptists of old, they look forward to the day when God's kingdom will come down from heaven. The message of the millennium is this: the kingly rule of God and of Christ is already among us. We should, therefore, direct our gaze downward, at history, where inside the course of sinful events the reign of Christ is actually taking place. The kingdom of God runs through our time and is moving towards its full manifestation in the return of Christ.

The vision of the thousand years of peace and justice is "the vision of the silver lining behind history. To us the clouds may appear ominously black and fearful, but from God's side it is quite different. Here is a vision that takes us right to the vestibule of eternity, to the very edge of those clouds, and allows us to peep behind them and see the backside of history to be the supernal reign of Jesus Christ" (Torrance, *Apocalypse*, p. 166).

All Things New

When God says, "I am making everything new" (Rev. 21:5), he does not announce anything new. This transformation is what the entire Bible is all about. It is what Jesus' miracles are all about. Each time Jesus performs a miracle he gives a preview of the new creation. Healing a blind or lame or deaf person is his way of letting us know that he intends to bring whatever is derailed back into line. Raising someone from the dead is his way of telling us that in the new creation "there will be no more death or mourning" (Rev. 21:4).

Jesus' parables too are about the new creation. They are windows offering a glimpse of the way in which all things are made new. The new creation comes in a way described in the parables. It comes "like a mustard seed, which a man took and planted in his field. Though it is the smallest of all your seeds, yet when it grows, it is the largest of garden plants and becomes a tree, so that the birds of the air come and perch in its branches" (Matt. 13:31-32). Again, the new creation is "like yeast that a woman took and mixed into a large amount of flour until it worked all through the dough" (Matt. 13:33).

Jesus' keen eye observes the sharp contrast between the beginning of everyday things and their end. In his parables he uses this contrast to illustrate what is true of the new creation. In its beginning stage it is apparently insignificant, but in its final stage it encompasses everything.

In his vision of the new creation John describes the indescribable. Therefore, he uses and negates descriptive terms proper to the old creation. The new creation is described by the ways it is *not* like the old.

No Sea

One outstanding feature of the new creation is the absence of the sea. "There was no longer any sea" (Rev. 21:1). This is not a word about the geography but about the demography of the new creation. In the book of Revelation the sea stands for the abyss out of which demonic forces rise to the surface. It is the home of the beast with ten horns and seven heads that utters blasphemies against God and is given temporary authority "over every tribe, people, language, and nation" and is worshiped by "every one whose name has not been written before the foundation of the world in the book of life of the Lamb that was slain" (Rev. 13:7f.).

In the new creation this sea will be no more.

No Temple

In the new creation there will be no temple, no specially reserved room for God. Instead, the whole world will be "room for God." The distinction between sacred and secular will have been done away with. The ancient prophecy will at last have come true: "On that day HOLY TO THE LORD will be inscribed on the bells of the horses" (Zech. 14:20). God will be all and in all. All will be subject to his will and do his will. The kingdom of this world will become "the kingdom of our Lord and of his Christ, and he will reign for ever and ever" (Rev. 11:15).

No Night

Night will not be part of the new creation, for it will have no need of sun or moon to shine upon it. The glory of God will be its light, and its lamp will be the Lamb (21:23). Nothing will eclipse the light that emanates from God. Though now we see in a mirror dimly, then we shall see face to face. Though now we know in part, then we shall understand fully.

"He who testifies to these things says, 'Yes, I am coming soon.' Amen. Come, Lord Jesus. The grace of the Lord Jesus be with God's people. Amen" (Rev. 22:20-21).

Eleven: God Reveals the Interior of History

Chapter Review Questions

1. In what different literary languages does the New Testament proclaim Jesus' ministry?

2. What characterizes apocalyptic language?

3. Is the book of Revelation an apocalypse?

4. What is the central message of Revelation?

5. What is the message of the millennium in Revelation 20?

General Discussion Questions

1. Why do the profoundest expressions of biblical faith, such as those in the book of Revelation, always come out of periods of catastrophe and agony and persecution?

2. As a way of becoming more familiar with apocalyptic language, try to describe a recent historical event the way an ancient apocalyptist might have done.

3. How does Revelation 1:4-5 offer a keyhole view of the entire book of Revelation?

4. Revelation 20:3 tells us that Satan is bound to keep him from deceiving the nations until the thousand years are ended. What does this mean?

Notes

Bibliography

The author acknowledges varying degrees of indebtedness to the following works:

Anderson, Bernhard W. *The Unfolding Drama of the Bible.* New York: Association Press, 1957.

Berkhof, Hendrikus, and Philip Potter. *Key Words of the Gospel.* London: SCM Press, 1964.

Bright, John. *A History of Israel.* Philadelphia: Westminster Press, 1959.

————. *Jeremiah* (The Anchor Bible). New York: Doubleday and Co., 1965.

————. *The Kingdom of God.* Nashville: Abingdon Press, 1953.

Buber, Martin. *Moses.* New York: Harper and Row, Pubs., Inc., 1960.

Childs, Brevard S. *The Book of Exodus.* Philadelphia: Westminster Press, 1974.

Cullman, Oscar. *Early Christian Worship.* Naperville, Ill.: Allenson, 1956.

Daube, David. *The Exodus Pattern in the Bible.* London: Faber and Faber, 1963.

Davies, W. D. *Invitation to the New Testament.* New York: Doubleday and Co., 1966.

————. *The New Creation.* Philadelphia: Fortress Press, 1971.

————. *Paul and Rabbinic Judaism.* London: S.P.C.K., 1955.

de Dietrich, Suzanne. *God's Unfolding Purpose.* Philadelphia: Westminster Press, 1960.

————. *The Witnessing Community.* Philadelphia: Westminster Press, 1958.

de Vaux, Roland. *Ancient Israel.* New York: McGraw-HIll Book Co., 1961.

Dodd, C.H. *The Meaning of Paul for Today.* London and Glasgow: Collins, 1958.

Ellul, Jacques. *Apocalypse.* New York: Seabury Press, 1977.

Freedman, David Noel, and James D. Smart. *God Has Spoken*. Philadelphia: Westminster Press, 1949.

Haenchen, Ernst. *The Acts of the Apostles*. Oxford: Basil Blackwell Pubs., Ltd., 1971.

Heschel, Abraham J. *The Prophets*. New York: Harper and Row, Pubs., Inc., 1962.

Holladay, William L. *Jeremiah: Spokesman Out of Time*. Philadelphia: Pilgrim Press, 1974.

Knight, George A. F. *Theology as Narration: A Commentary on the Book of Exodus*. Grand Rapids: Wm. B. Eerdmans Pub. Co., 1976.

Lane, William L. *The Gospel According to Mark* (The New International Commentary on the New Testament). Grand Rapids: Wm. B. Eerdmans Pub. Co., 1975.

Lilje, Hanns. *The Last Book of the Bible*. Translated by Olive Wyan. Philadelphia: Fortress Press, 1967.

Morris, Leon. *Apocalyptic*. Grand Rapids: Wm. B. Eerdmans Pub. Co., 1972.

Muilenburg, James. *The Way of Israel*. New York: Harper and Row, Pubs., Inc., 1961.

Napier, B. Davie. *From Faith to Faith*. New York: Harper and Row, Pubs., Inc., 1955.

Perrin, Norman. *The Resurrection according to Matthew, Mark, and Luke*. Philadelphia: Fortress Press, 1977.

Ramsey, Michael. *The Resurrection of Christ*. Rev. ed. Glasgow: Collins, 1961.

Richardson, Alan. *Genesis I-XI*. London: SCM Press, 1953.

Ridderbos, Herman N. *Matthew's Witness to Jesus Christ*. New York: Association Press, 1958.

————. *When the Time Had Fully Come*. Grand Rapids: Wm. B. Eerdmans Pub. Co., 1957.

Rowley, H. H. *The Relevance of Apocalyptic*. New York: Association Press, 1964.

Rylaarsdam, J. Coert. *The Proverbs, Ecclesiastes, the Son of Solomon* (Layman's Bible Commentary). Vol. 10. Richmond: John Knox Press, 1964.

Sanders, James A. *The Old Testament in the Cross*. New York: Harper and Row, Pubs., Inc., 1961.

Sanders, Paul S., ed. *Twentieth Century Interpretations of the Book of Job*. Englewood Cliffs, N.J.: Prentice-Hall, Inc., 1968.

Scott, R. B. Y. *The Relevance of the Prophets*. New York: Macmillan Publishing Co., 1944.

————. *The Way of Wisdom.* New York: Macmillan Publishing Co., 1971.

Smart, James D. *Doorway to a New Age: A Study of Paul's Letter to the Romans.* Philadelphia: Westminster Press, 1972.

Torrance, Thomas F. *The Apocalypse Today.* London: Camelot Press, 1960.

von Rad, Gerhard. *God at Work in Israel.* Nashville: Abingdon Press, 1980.

————. *Moses.* London: Lutterworth Press, 1960.

————. *Old Testament Theology.* London: Oliver and Boyd, 1962 and 1965.

————. *The Problem of the Hexateuch and Other Essays.* London: Oliver and Boyd, 1966.

————. *Wisdom in Israel.* Nashville: Abingdon Press, 1972.

Westermann, Claus. *A Thousand Years and a Day.* Philadelphia: Fortress Press, 1966.